The Mysteries of Fire and Water

Translated from the French
Original title: «LES RÉVÉLATIONS DU FEU ET DE L'EAU»

Original edition
© 1991, Éditions Prosveta S.A., France, ISBN 2-85566-496-9

© 1993, Éditions Prosveta S.A., France, ISBN 2-85566-545-0

ISBN 2-85566-545-0

Omraam Mikhaël Aïvanhov

The Mysteries of Fire and Water

Izvor Collection – No. 232

P R O S V E T A

Readers are asked to note that Omraam Mikhaël Aïvanhov's teaching was exclusively oral. This volume includes passages from several different lectures all dealing with the same theme.

TABLE OF CONTENTS

Chapter One

THE TWO PRINCIPLES OF CREATION, WATER AND FIRE

At the beginning of the book of *Genesis* Moses gives an account of the creation of the world in which he enumerates the different elements of the universe – sun, moon, stars, vegetation, animals and human beings – and describes how they came to be. But he also says something whose deepest significance can be understood only by an initiate. He says, '*And the Spirit of God hovered over the waters.*' Why over the waters? Because water represents the original cosmic matter that was penetrated and fertilized by primordial fire, the Spirit of God. Contrary to popular belief, the element that best expresses and manifests the properties and qualities of matter is not earth but water, for those qualities are receptivity, adaptability and plasticity.

Water, then, symbolizes the primal matter that was fecundated by the seed of the spirit; water is the matrix, the womb of life. Life was born of water thanks to the principle of fire, for there can be no life without the intervention of fire; it was fire that animated this primal matter and set it in motion. Of itself, water, matter, does not possess life; life has to be infused into it by fire. Life on earth came into existence through the action of fire on water. The first germs of life were brought to earth by the sun's rays which reached the water of the world's oceans; and that water, like a loving mother, received those germs of life and continued to nourish them with the light and warmth of the sun.

Once we understand that water symbolizes the universal matter from which the cosmos was created, we can more easily interpret Moses' account of how God separated the waters above from the waters below: *'Then God said, Let there be a firmament in the midst of the waters, and let it divide the waters from the waters. Thus God made the firmament, and divided the waters which were under the firmament from the waters which were above the firmament; and it was so. And God called the firmament Heaven.'* The waters above the firmament, which are known in initiatic science as Astral Light or the Great Magic Agent, represent the primordial ocean in which all creatures are immersed and in which they find the nourishment they need. One might almost say that it is in order to remind us of these primordial waters that a baby is immersed before birth in the amniotic fluid in its mother's womb. We are all immersed in the immensity of the cosmos just as fish are immersed in the sea, but as the entrances to our inner being are so often clogged with impurities we are not nourished and vivified as we should be by the waters that enfold us.

Water and fire, therefore, represent the two principles of creation, and their action in the universe is symbolized by the cross, a symbol which, as you know, is found in all civilizations and which is very rich in meaning. The horizontal line of the cross represents the action of the feminine principle, water. The natural tendency of this principle is to extend outwards, to spread as widely as possible over the surface and to disappear underground through every available crack or crevice. The vertical line represents the masculine principle, fire, and this principle tends, on the contrary, to restrict its movements on the horizontal plane and to expand upwards. Water, therefore, relates to breadth and depth, whereas fire relates to height. These two directions, horizontality and verticality, of which the cross is the synthesis, are the best expression of the action of the masculine and feminine principles in creation as a whole, as well as in all creatures. The universe is full of this symbol.

To most Christians the cross is simply a reminder of the death of Jesus, they do not realize that by limiting it to this they are stripping it of most of its significance. No one can deny that the death of Jesus on the cross was an event of considerable importance in the history of mankind, but the symbolism of the cross far exceeds that one event, and if you make the effort to penetrate its meaning in the light of the lesson contained in the two principles, water and fire, it will put you within reach of the greatest mysteries of creation. As far as I am concerned, I can tell you that nothing has been of greater importance in my life than water and fire. The memories of childhood that have left the deepest mark on me are all associated with water and fire.

I was born in a village in Macedonia, at the foot of the *Babouna Planina* (Grandmother's Mountain), whose highest peak was Mount Pelister. I still remember some of the events that occurred during the few years I spent in that village, and one of my most vivid memories is of a discovery I made when I was four or five years old. Not far from our house I found a spring of water. The clear, transparent water bubbling out of the ground made such an impression on me that I stayed there watching it for hours on end. The image of that spring is still so vivid in my mind's eye that even now, when I picture it again, I experience the same sense of wonder and delight that I experienced as a child. I have often asked myself what it was about that water that made such a deep impression on me at such an early age. But water was not the only thing that made an impression on me; I was also fascinated by fire. The only problem was that fire was more dangerous because, of course, when I wanted to see a fire, I had to light one! My family soon learned never to leave a box of matches within my reach!

Why was I so fascinated by water and fire? Because water and fire are the most beautiful, potent and significant expressions that nature has to offer of the two great cosmic principles, the masculine and the feminine. Also because I was destined to spend my life studying and working with them. As a matter of fact, if it were possible to make a detailed study of different people's lives, you would certainly find that many of the impressions, experiences or behaviour apparent in their childhood foreshadowed their principal interests and the areas in which they would have to work in their later lives.

You will perhaps be thinking that no one had ever told you that water and fire were so important. Well, this shows that you have not read the Gospels carefully, particularly the account in *St John's Gospel* of the conversation between Jesus and Nicodemus. Nicodemus was a doctor of law who came by night to talk to Jesus. It was to him that Jesus gave the answer that has intrigued so many theologians since: *'Most assuredly, I say to you, unless a man is born of water and the spirit, he cannot enter the kingdom of God.'* There is a certain correspondence between these words and the passage from *Genesis* that we talked about earlier: *'And the spirit of God hovered over the waters.'* In both instances it is the phenomenon of birth that is involved – the birth of the universe and the spiritual birth of man – and in both instances we find the same elements, fire (the spirit) and water (matter). Just as the universe is born of fire and water, man must be born of spiritual fire and water in order to enter into the higher state of consciousness that we call the kingdom of God, for on the spiritual plane fire is wisdom and water is love. Those few words to Nicodemus are enough to show us that Jesus also possessed this science of water and fire, the science of the two great cosmic principles.

The spontaneous direction of water and fire are, as we have already seen, diametrically opposite: fire tends to rise within narrow limits, to make its flames converge towards a single goal, whereas water flows downwards and, in descending, tends to spread outwards. And yet if you watch closely it is possible to see a certain similarity in the movements of the two elements. Have you ever noticed how the movement of a waterfall resembles that of a fire in reverse? And the flames of a fire are like a waterfall flowing upwards to its source. A few years ago one of our sisters filmed some waterfalls and gave me the film, and while I was showing it to the brothers and sisters, I projected it in reverse, just to see the effect. It was quite extraordinary: the movement of the water was exactly the same as that of fire! If you ever have a chance to try this do so, and you will see for yourself. It is as though water were a condensation of fire flowing down into the bowels of the earth, and fire were water leaping up to the heavens. It is as though fire and water were one and the same substance manifesting itself in two different aspects.

It is precisely these two aspects that are so instructive. One of the things they teach us is that there are two different approaches to knowledge: the horizontal approach, which spreads its investigations over a broad area, and the vertical approach, which consists in detaching oneself from the surface and seeking truth on a higher level. The first method is that of water, the second that of fire.

He who chooses the method of water must be prepared for a long and painful apprenticeship. You all know what an adventurous life water has: it flows through all sorts and kinds of terrain, picking up silt and impurities along the way, before sinking into the dark regions under the ground where it is subjected to tremendous pressure. No, the fate of water as it flows over or under the earth is not always enviable. Anyone who follows this path is bound to suffer and be faced with difficult conditions. He will be jostled and beaten, ill-treated and broken by circumstances, and by the time he reaches the end of his peregrinations and is able to say, 'I understand; I have learned my lesson,' he will often be in a very sorry state. That is all right; it does not really matter, because at least he will have understood. There is much to be said for the method of water therefore. But the method of fire is far preferable, for it tears you away from your earthly conditions and launches you aloft; you enter the realm of light, and light immediately reveals all knowledge to you.

When Jesus said, *'Be wise as serpents and harmless as doves,'* he was saying that we have to know how to use both methods: the method of water (symbolized by the serpent which Moses described as being more cunning than any beast of the field), and the method of fire (the dove). These then are the two paths of knowledge. The serpent slithering along the ground represents the horizontal, sinuous movement of water, and the dove soaring upwards in flight represents the upward movement of fire. The knowledge of the dove is the knowledge of fire, that of the Holy Spirit; it illuminates us.

Just as fire and water are opposed by reason of the direction of their flow, they are also opposed by reason of their nature. If you attempt to unite fire and water they will destroy each other. To all appearances therefore they are bitter enemies; water, from which life springs, can extinguish fire, and fire, which also gives birth to life, can make water disappear by evaporation. If you want them to work together you must not throw water directly on to the fire; you have to find a way of adjusting them to each other, a way of reconciling the two forces. How? By putting your water in a saucepan and putting the saucepan on the fire. The water will start to move and expand and boil; it will push against the walls that hold it prisoner and try to get out, protesting that it needs more space. Where was all that energy hiding before it began to emerge from the boiling water? It was already in the water, but it is fire that liberates it. Fire will not kill water if the two are kept at a respectful distance from each other, therefore; on the contrary, fire exalts water and brings out all it potentialities which can then be put to work.

In reality, then, fire and water are not enemies, far from it; they show great affection for each other just as long as there is a partition of some kind between them, otherwise it is open warfare. Fire says to water, 'Keep well away from me, or you will extinguish me!' And water says to fire, 'Go away, or you will reduce me to steam!' But if you put a partition between them you will hear them murmuring sweet words of love to each other. Have you never enjoyed listening to a conversation between water and fire? Take the time one day to listen to the sound of boiling water.

Inventors, engineers and mechanics know how to put water to work in machines by using fire to release the power contained in it. Yes, but although they are very good at making physical fire and water work for them in their kitchens or factories, when it comes to their own personal lives they are not so skilful; they do not know how to use fire to exalt water. In fact they often mix the two together, with the result that they lose both.

You can see instances of this in many married couples: the man represents fire and the woman water, and because they are too ignorant to think about keeping some kind of partition (symbolically speaking) between them, the husband loses all his ardour, his fire is extinguished, while the wife evaporates and dries up. Now, I know that you are wondering what kind of partition I am talking about: first and foremost it is a question of a man and woman being conscious that when they unite, it should not be for the sake of pleasure, but in order to work together for a common ideal. Only if this consciousness exists can the union between a man and woman be creative. If it is absent their union will inevitably be mutually destructive. Yes, it is not enough to observe the transformations undergone by water and know how to make use of them technologically, we must also apply the lesson they teach to our personal life, and above all to our spiritual life.

We all know the different states of water: solid (when it turns to ice), liquid, and gaseous (when it turns to steam). And we all know that it is fire, the degree of fire or heat, that determines these different states. Fire transforms water into steam, and in so doing symbolizes the spirit that acts on matter to transform it and make it lighter, subtler and purer. This is why we can liken a human being to a saucepan of water that is being heated on a fire. The only difference is that, in my example, the fire is underneath, whereas the spirit is above, but the result is the same. Any life there may be inside the saucepan is there because of the work of the spirit. And when a person dies, 'the saucepan' still exists, but nothing moves within it because the fire is no longer there. What do you think of my comparison? Excellent, isn't it? Or perhaps I should say mouth-watering, since we are talking about saucepans!

Fire, then, is a symbol of the spirit, of the masculine principle that acts on water, which is the symbol of matter, and we all possess this fire. This means that we can all apply this law to our own inner lives by exposing all the crude, sordid matter of our faults and failings to the spiritual sun so that they melt and disintegrate in its heat. And this is also the science of alchemy.

Chapter Two

THE SECRET OF COMBUSTION

Fire reveals life's greatest mystery to us, the mystery of combustion. For that is what life is, combustion. Every manifestation in the universe necessarily requires energy, and that energy can only be produced by the combustion of matter. This is a rule that applies equally to man himself: we eat and breathe, but we also think and feel emotions, and all these actions entail combustion. As a matter of fact, there is a popular saying that expresses this quite vividly: when someone both works and plays to excess we say that he is burning the candle at both ends. But the fact that most people know and use this expression does not mean that they pay much attention to the way they use their energies; on the contrary, there is so much disorder in their lives that they constantly burn their candle at both ends. They imagine that the supply of energy is inexhaustible, that it will automatically be replenished. Unfortunately not! True, certain elements can be replaced because cosmic intelligence has designed the human organism in such a way that it can repair and replace some of what it uses as it goes along. But when someone behaves unreasonably he can never make up all his losses.

Those who live in a state of disorder and passion waste their most precious energies, and in doing so not only do they deprive their psychic and spiritual bodies of nourishment, but they also undermine the health of their physical bodies. Something always has to be burned in order to sustain life. The great question is, what must be burned? It is fire itself that gives us the answer. When you want to build a fire you start by collecting some dry sticks, some dead, black twigs and branches which you lay in the fireplace. When you first see those dead branches there is no beauty in them, but once they are ablaze, what a beautiful, splendid show of light! All that dead wood that might have lain there abandoned and useless has been transformed by fire into light, heat and energy.

You will say, 'Yes, we understand that, but has this dead wood got anything to do with us?' It has indeed! Symbolically speaking, there is a lot of dead wood in you. You too have piles of black, dead branches within you which could be thrown on the fire and burned. All your selfish, passionate impulses, all the manifestations of your lower nature are so much dead wood, and if you throw them on to the fire they too will produce light and heat. This is what we mean by sacrifice. You must learn to burn all your jealousy, anger and sensuality; in this way not only will you be rid of them, but at the same time the light in your mind and the warmth in your heart will become brighter and more intense. Those who are afraid to sacrifice any of their instincts and lusts will remain forever in spiritual cold and darkness. Without sacrifice there can be no fire. But none of this need alarm you; you have enormous reserves of dead wood waiting to be burned. Your lower nature is a gigantic tree which contains enough fuel to provide you with all the light and heat you need, and ensure the activity of all your spiritual centres for hundreds of years to come.

Unfortunately most human beings cherish their lower nature and try to keep it intact. They refuse to be consumed by fire, so they lie scattered over the ground like so many dead and broken branches waiting to be set alight. They are going to have to endure great tribulations and suffer great disappointments and bereavements before they finally make up their minds to collect all that old stuff that has been piling up within them for centuries and throw it on the fire. At the moment they still hesitate; they are terrified of making the sacrifice because they see it as a deprivation, a loss, an impoverishment. And this shows that they have not understood the first thing about it. Of course there will be something that disappears, but that is precisely the point; some things have to disappear so that other, better things may appear, so that light and warmth may appear. You will say, 'Yes, but a tree cannot go on burning indefinitely; there is soon nothing left of it.' True, but man can burn indefinitely. In fact, once he has been set alight he can no longer be extinguished; there will always be plenty of matter in him to feed the fire.

True sacrifice is the process by which all our old, worn-out, impure elements are transformed into light and heat, that is to say, into love and wisdom. It is because initiates understand this that they offer themselves up every day to the Angel of Fire so that they may be devoured and consumed. Men have often compared God to a consuming fire but they do not really know very much about this fire; all they know is that it burns so fiercely that man cannot bear it. This is the pure fire of the Spirit; at its touch all forms melt and disappear. Those who receive the kiss of this fire melt and blend into it to become one flame.

A great many people have written very complicated books about the experiences of mystics. But the truth is not complicated; it is really very simple. The experience of a mystic is the experience of fire, of the sacred fire that he feeds by throwing bits of his lower nature onto it every day, just as we throw sticks and dead branches onto the fires in our hearths. Look at a log fire: all the branches and twigs that were once separate and scattered are brought together to form a single flame, a blaze of light and heat; they are all obliged to think and feel as the fire thinks and feels.

Consider the planets spinning round the sun; what do they do? They too sacrifice themselves and help to feed the sun's fire. The fire of the sun is the focus, the point of convergence for all the energies and emanations of the invisible entities that inhabit our solar system. The sun is the hearth, the altar of sacrifice. All these entities nourish and sustain the sacred fire of the sun, so that not only they themselves but the whole universe benefits from their sacrifice. Of course the fuel they throw on the fire is not the same as ours; they have no dead branches to burn. But it is not the nature of what these entities cast on the fire that concerns us. What concerns us is that we must feed the divine fire within us, and we can only do this by sacrificing our inferior instincts and appetites and all the manifestations of our lower nature.

What else can fire teach us? Look at a bonfire and you will see that the branches on top of the pile seem to burn more quickly and with more eagerness than those below. It is as though they were in a great hurry because they are so happy to be transformed into light, into sparks of fire. The branches beneath them burn much more slowly, more reluctantly. And those that fall off the pile and roll away from the fire seem to be uncertain of what to do. They are wondering whether they really want to be burned or not. If they hesitate it is because they have moved away from the fire, and it is never good to stray too far. They continue to blaze for a little while and then the flames die down and the fire goes out. So as you see, even a bonfire gives us a portrait of life: those who rise burn brightly, those who stay down below smoulder and stagnate, and those who fall away are extinguished.

The mystery of fire is the mystery of life. The fire in man is the spark of life that dwells in his heart. At the exact moment when this spark leaves his heart a man dies. This is why the one thing that matters is to learn how to protect this fire, not only physically but, above all, spiritually.

Chapter Three

WATER, THE MATRIX OF LIFE

Water is the vital fluid of the earth. Rivers and streams represent the arteries and veins of the earth, the lakes represent its plexuses, and so on. Like blood, water is a priceless, indispensable element which nourishes and brings life to all creatures – rocks, plants, animals and men. Even crystals need water in order to be formed; crystals and precious stones can exist only if a few particles of water are present in their composition. Without this water they crumble into dust. It is the water that gives gems their hardness, their colour and their translucent character. And vegetation, which has its roots buried in the soil, is the etheric body of the earth. Yes, trees are the earth's etheric body, and water is the fluid that sustains the life of this body. Flowers, trees and plants fashion and vivify the earth through the medium of water.

If you want to penetrate the secrets of nature you must try to understand the importance of water. You must meditate on what it means, on its properties and its power, on all that is concealed within it. People are very neglectful of water; they have no real appreciation of it, no understanding of its worth. You will object that, on the contrary, you are very aware of the importance of water. Yes, on the instinctive, mechanical, unconscious level that is true, but that is not what I am talking about. I am talking about an appreciation of water that must grow and develop in your consciousness and become a potent factor in your psychic, emotional and mental life.

I have seen people who are capable of standing and gazing at a river, a lake or the ocean with no more emotion than if they were gazing at a wall. The water means nothing to them; they behave as though it were not there. The only time they are concerned with water is when there is a shortage; then they worry about how they are going to cook, wash themselves or the dishes, and water the garden. It is really amazing! What will it take to wake them up, to get them to discover the beauty of water and to express some feeling for it, some appreciation of it? How can anyone fail to be moved, to feel an inner tremor of joy at the sight of this limpid matter, at the sight of this manifestation of the feminine principle, of the sublime Mother who enfolds us in her purity and light? They must be blind! Are these the people who imagine that they are going to penetrate the mysteries of the universe?

It is time you began to understand the important part that water plays in nature and made up your minds to work with it in order to transform your inner life. It is all very well to enjoy walking beside a river or a waterfall, to appreciate a drink of fresh spring water, or go for a swim in a lake or in the sea, but you are not really working when you do that. You will never produce the slightest change in your inner life unless and until you learn to communicate with water, until you begin to talk to it and make friends with it.

The first condition that has to be fulfilled if you want to make friends with water is to approach it with respect. You must realize that water is the home of many pure and beautiful entities who will not look kindly on you if you fail to show some love and consideration for them. If you want to go for a swim for instance, especially if it is in a lake, you must not do so carelessly; you must take the trouble to put yourself in a suitable frame of mind. Start by asking the entities that live in that water for their permission to bathe in it, because when you do so it is as though you were washing away your impurities in the water in which they live, and as you can understand, this could be very disagreeable for them. Be careful and considerate therefore.

However, as you may not often have the opportunity to practise making contact with water in a natural setting, it is still possible to do so at home. You only need a cup or bowl of water, for even such a tiny quantity can represent all the waters of the earth. Symbolically, magically, a single drop of water is enough to establish a link between yourself and all the rivers and oceans of the world. Take your bowl of water therefore, concentrate on it and speak to it so that it becomes even more vibrant and full of life. Tell it how beautiful it is, how much you admire it and how grateful you would be if it would give you some of its purity and transparency. Then you can touch it and pour it over your hands, for instance, with the thought that you are communicating with its etheric body and absorbing its vibrations, that it is impregnating your whole being.

Or you can dip your hands in the water and conjure up a picture of a lake of pure, crystal-clear water high up in the mountains; you can see yourself bathing in that water and receiving its freshness and purity into yourself. If you do this with the consciousness of doing something sacred you will feel your being vibrating in harmony with the whole of nature; you will feel that you are lighter and purer, that even your brain functions more efficiently. Yes, such an exercise can effect tremendous changes, on condition, of course, that the most potent factor, your conscious mind, is focused on what you are doing. Thanks to your powers of thought you can use everything that God has created to help you to become better, purer, stronger and more intelligent.

Repeat exercises of this kind often. Gaze at some water in a crystal bowl, touch it lovingly, feel its coolness and softness, contemplate its transparency – all this may seem pointless and insignificant, but it is not; and since, of the four elements, water is the one that mingles most closely with our own organism, by drinking it we can communicate with the pure forces of the universe and absorb the elements it contains. If you want to do this, of course, you must not gulp it down, you must sip it slowly, remembering that you are imbibing the blood of nature, the sap that is food and drink for all creatures. This is all quite new to you, I am sure! Has anyone ever told you before how to drink water in such a way that it will communicate its life, its purity and its transparency to you?

Only someone who has fainted from thirst in the desert can really understand what water is. Water is the mother of life and we owe it respect, gratitude and love. At the marriage feast of Cana Jesus transformed water into wine, that is to say, into blood, into life. When you drink some water you should remember that this water will be transformed into life-giving blood within your body. Meditate at length on this idea and ask the water that nurtures all creatures to reveal the secrets of eternal life to you.

Chapter Four

CIVILIZATION, A PRODUCT OF WATER

What is a civilization? It is a product of water. If this idea surprises you, you only have to consider the fact that from time immemorial men have always made their homes near water. Sometimes they settled on the seashore, but more often beside a lake or on the banks of a river. Why is this? The answer is simple.

Water comes from a spring in the mountains and flows downwards, twisting and turning between the rocks in its path, and mosses, grasses and flowers start to grow alongside it. Gradually, as it gouges a bed out of the earth and other streams join it, it becomes a broad, deep river; trees grow beside it, and fishes, insects, birds and little animals live in it and along its banks. Finally, when it reaches the plains and men see the life that abounds along its banks, they too are drawn to it; it gives them the conditions they need for their own settlements. So now you understand: wherever there is water, vegetation, animals and human beings appear. Suppose people said, 'Let us put some birds here, some fruit trees over there, a school here', and so on, without first of all making sure that there was some water, the birds would fly away, the trees would die and the school would have to be closed.

Of course the water I am talking about is symbolic: it is love. Water, life, love... they are one and the same. The levels on which they exist are different, but the reality is the same. In the absence of love there can only be a desert, and nobody wants to settle down in a desert. People cross a desert but they do not live in it; they keep moving on until they find an oasis with water. Unfortunately most people never think about water – that is to say, love – when they want to build something. They rely exclusively on organization, thinking that love is unnecessary. They establish programmes, draw up rules and regulations, put up buildings and distribute offices and functions to a lot of people; and it is all magnificent... but it is a desert! And I can assure you that not many people are willing to remain any length of time in a desert, no matter how well organized it is.

As long as life is absent nothing can really work, for life is the true motor behind every venture. But as soon as life – that is to say, love – appears, even if nothing is organized the rest begins to take shape around it, just as vegetation, animals and human beings gather along the banks of a river. This is something that I have always known and it is the reason why I have never bothered about organization. My work has been to let the water flow, and in this way, little by little, the Brotherhood was born and started to grow. And this is what you must do too: start by letting the water flow.

Sometimes a person will come to me complaining that he is lost and confused: 'I do not know what is the matter with me. I feel empty; I have no more inspiration, no interest in anything any more!' When I look at him I can see that, as he says, he has no idea why he is in such a pitiful state. I have to explain it to him. 'The reason is simply that you have cut off the flow of water from the spring.' 'What spring?' he asks. 'I haven't cut anything off! 'Yes, I am afraid you have. Nothing flows within you any more; and when the flow of water is cut off the grass and flowers shrivel and die, and the birds fly away. Even human beings stop coming to such a sad, empty place.' The grass, flowers and birds are your feelings, thoughts and emotions, with all their different forms, colours, scents and songs. Just because someone has betrayed or disappointed you, you close your heart to others and let all your love and enthusiasm die. This is not a very intelligent reaction; in fact it has a double disadvantage: it does nothing to change the things that have upset you so much, and it deprives you yourself of something valuable.

Whatever difficulties and distress you have to endure, you must keep the water flowing from your spring, for that is the only way to become rich; rich because of all the entities that will come and embellish your life with their presence. If you find yourself in a desert it is no good complaining about it; it is you who got yourself there. No one else is to blame. I know you think that it is not your fault; that it is the fault of whoever deceived and betrayed you. You think that it is they who condemned you to live in a desert. No, you are wrong; no one has forced you to be in such a state. To be sure, people may have tried to injure you, but you do not have to accept their viciousness passively, and, above all you do not have to do yourself an even greater injury by allowing your spring to run dry. If you do not put things right, if you just let go of hope, love and faith you will be dead. Yes, even before you die you will be dead.

Your spring must never stop flowing. 'But people will always use me and take advantage of me. I shall be an eternal victim!' Perhaps, but to be slighted and betrayed is a far lesser evil than to allow your spring to run dry, for then you lose everything. To be sure, it is important to know how to channel the flow of water and not allow it to run in all directions, into any and every garden. To say that you must allow it to flow does not mean that it is forbidden to protect it. I have never said that you must distribute the treasures of your heart and soul to all and sundry without discrimination. I am simply warning you that to close your heart against other human beings, on the pretext that some of them have betrayed and disappointed you, is an attitude that is fatal to your own happiness. It is for your own happiness that I say this because, unfortunately, you do not know what to do in order to be happy.

From now on, therefore, meditate more often on the image of running water and try to understand how many blessings it can bring you.

Chapter Five

THE LIVING CHAIN OF SUN, EARTH AND WATER

Water does not flow only on the surface of the earth; it also flows under the earth, where its emanations are, as it were, the elixir of life that nourishes the mineral, vegetable and animal kingdoms. If water did not also flow in the bowels of the earth there would be no stones or plants, no animals, and no human beings.

You will ask, 'What purpose does the sun's energy serve if, as you say, it is the subterranean influences that nurture life on earth ?' It is quite simple: the sun does not give its energies directly to the creatures on earth; it gives them first of all to the earth itself, to the planet, and the earth transmits them to the creatures that inhabit it. For the earth is alive, and as I have often told you, its etheric body reaches thousands of miles out into space. The real surface of the earth is very far away from what we normally think of as its surface; the earth's crust on which we walk is simply the physical, material husk of the planet. The different layers of the earth's atmosphere are not part of cosmic space, they belong to earth. The atmosphere is the skin of the planet, and currents of cosmic energy from outer space penetrate this skin and are transformed on contact with it. In other words, the atmosphere acts as a filter and allows only elements that are beneficial to life on earth to pass through it. The cosmic currents that penetrate the atmosphere are then picked up by the peaks of mountains, which act as antennae or aerials, and when the snow and ice on those summits melt, the water that flows down over the earth and filters through the geological layers under the earth is impregnated with these currents. Rain water too contains energies from the higher levels of the atmosphere.

The energy that nourishes plants, animals and human beings, therefore, is solar energy, but solar energy that has first been absorbed, transformed and redistributed by the planet. From this point of view the earth is as important as the sun. You must not think that when you expose your body to the sun you are receiving its rays directly; before the sun's rays reach you they have had to pass through the earth's atmosphere, and it is because the earth's atmosphere has transformed them that you are able to receive and absorb them. This is why it is important always to be in harmony with the earth; to love and respect it. Otherwise, even if you expose yourself to the sun's rays you will benefit much less from its light and heat.

You should study this living chain of sun, earth and water. Rivers and streams are the lines of communication that link the plains and valleys to the mountain peaks, and the mountain peaks are like hungry mouths, waiting to drink and absorb energies from the cosmos. Mountains are transformers of cosmic energy, and the subterranean waters that flow through them become impregnated with this energy and pass it on to the different kingdoms of nature.

The ancients were not altogether wrong in considering that it was the earth, not the sun, which was the centre of the universe. For human beings it is the earth, their planet, that is the most important; it is the earth that is truly their universe, and the centre of the earth is the centre of that universe. From a certain point of view, therefore, you can say that the geocentric system of Ptolemy was as true as the heliocentric system of Copernicus! Yes, because human beings do not receive energy directly from the sun; it is the earth that receives it and transmits it to them. And besides, the growth and development of human beings follows the rhythm of the earth. They cannot evolve faster than their planet, for the collective destiny of mankind is subject to the evolution of the earth. Only a few rare beings who are specially advanced can detach themselves from the whole and evolve more rapidly.

Chapter Six

A BLACKSMITH WORKS WITH FIRE

If we are unsuccessful in our efforts to change our inner form it is because, symbolically speaking, we never leave the realm of earth, and the cold that prevails on earth congeals and stiffens forms. If we want to soften and remodel our inner forms we must enter the realm of fire. Inner reality follows the same pattern as outer, physical reality. Everyone knows that before trying to hammer a piece of iron into shape a blacksmith has to make it soft and malleable by plunging it into fire. If the iron is not red-hot, the blows of the hammer will either make no impression at all or will simply break the piece of iron. And this is what many people do to themselves: they try to transform themselves without having plunged themselves in spiritual fire, with the result that either nothing changes or they do such violence to their nervous system that it breaks down completely.

Now let me draw a lesson from the way a blacksmith works and show you the great initiatic secrets contained in the way he uses fire. He starts by thrusting a piece of metal into the fire and waiting for it to become first red, and then white and incandescent. We can see how, without destroying anything, the fire gradually communicates its own heat and light to the metal. A piece of cold, dull grey iron becomes as hot, luminous and radiant as the fire itself, and as it is gradually transformed it acquires new properties.

A human being can be compared to a piece of iron: he can only be transformed by fire – by spiritual fire. Just as physical fire has the power to make metal sufficiently malleable for the blacksmith to give it a new shape, the celestial fire of divine love has the power to plunge man into a spiritual state in which he discards his old, opaque, ungainly form and acquires one that is new and radiantly luminous. This truth has always been known to true mystics and initiates. They have always known how to find the true fire that resides in the soul and the spirit, and to immerse themselves in it. In this way they became so perfectly malleable that they could then wield the hammer of thought to beat themselves into new shapes, and finally temper the newly forged metal so that it would retain its form.

And here too is a detail which needs to be interpreted. In order to make a new form tough and durable the blacksmith plunges the red-hot metal into cold water. This is the cold water of the trials and difficulties we encounter in life, for it is our trials that temper us and make us strong. It is not enough to experience moments of ecstasy in prayer and contemplation, to experience union with the world of light; these states must be made to last, and this can only be achieved by subjecting them to the trials of everyday life. We speak about forging character, and it is precisely this that forges character: the ordeals and obstacles it has to overcome. Make no mistake about it, it is not because you have tasted a few sublime moments of communion with heaven, in which you felt that you understood and were in control of everything, that you can expect to be spared any further tribulations. No, you will not be spared; on the contrary, it is thanks to those tribulations that your new inner form will become tough and durable.

In order to change the shape of your inner being then, you must try to enter the realm of fire, that is to say, the realm of the spirit. Try to make your moments of prayer and meditation last as long as possible so as to model and mould yourself anew. If you refuse to do this work yourself you will have to burn and be softened by the fire of suffering, until you finally make up your mind to change. For cosmic Intelligence does not allow human beings to stagnate. If they refuse to work with divine fire to achieve their own transformation they are obliged to endure the fire of suffering. Why are you afflicted by certain vicious tendencies, certain mental terrors or physical illnesses? Because you did not know these truths in your past lives, so you lived foolishly, and all the accumulated errors of the past have solidified within you like tumours, and you are faced today with a tough, tenacious matter that defies your attempts to transform it. What can you do about it? You can set in motion the reverse process by dissolving these tumours in the fire of the spirit, and by creating new, purer, and more harmonious forms and expressions.

In order to transform ourselves, in order to remodel our temperament, our innate tendencies, our habits, and even our heredity, we must call on the fire of heaven and implore it to come into our being. And when it comes we must keep fanning it until it melts us. And then, by means of our thoughts, we must work tirelessly to hammer out new forms within ourselves. There, that is how I interpret the work of a blacksmith.

I have personally experienced all that I have been talking about today. I have known this fire. Perhaps I do not speak with the learning of those who have written books about the raptures and ecstasies of mystics, but I have experienced these raptures and ecstasies for myself. I have had the joy and privilege of being allowed to taste this fire, and have seen that it can melt and refashion all our old, time-hardened forms. This is why we must wish for nothing but this heavenly fire; we must think of and contemplate this fire until it inflames and transforms our hearts and souls, our whole being. Do not rely on other people's explanations or writings; they can do nothing for you as long as this fire is not in you.

So trust me, and make up your minds that you are going to get to know the power of heavenly fire, that you are going to feel it and possess it within you. In order to achieve this you must concentrate deeply, far more deeply, on the sun and on the fire that fills the universe. Try to understand the nature of this fire; try to understand its power to enter into us, to stir the very depths of our being, to communicate its own properties to us. Learn to draw it into yourself and soak it up, so that the old forms that have hardened within you become soft and pliable and ready to be remodelled.

Chapter Seven

WATER IS BORN OF MOUNTAINS

Mountains serve as immense aerials by means of which the earth communicates with heaven. And it is because water takes its source in the mountains that it is so precious, for it is impregnated by heavenly fluids. If you want to understand the wealth and power of water you must know its birthplace: mountains. Any geography book will tell you all you want to know about mountains in terms of climate, vegetation, and so on, but for my part I shall tell you only what they represent for our spiritual life.

During the twenty years I spent with the Master Peter Deunov in Bulgaria, mountains occupied a very prominent place in my life. Every summer the Master would bring together the whole Brotherhood in the Rila Mountains. We would stay up there for several weeks, sometimes two months, depending on the weather. During the rest of the year the Master and many of the brothers and sisters lived in Sofia, but even then we used to spend almost every weekend in the mountains, for

Mount Vitocha is only a few miles from the town. Sometimes we would stay up there for several days, and thanks to the Master, we always came back from those days in the mountains loaded with heavenly gifts, for it was he who taught us the attitude we should have towards nature, towards streams and rocks, lakes, waterfalls and mountain peaks. From the moment we set out until we got home again the Master would use each of these as an occasion to teach us something.

On the day we were to leave we would assemble at Izgrev and there, before giving the signal to start walking, the Master, who was always vigilant and alert, would quietly make contact with the invisible world. When he took the first step it was as though he was setting out with us on a marvellous adventure. He would explain to us how important it was to have the right inner attitude and the right intentions when taking the first step. Everything depends on the how and when of that first step. The Master always looked carefully to right and left before starting to walk. He would begin walking slowly and gradually increase his pace until we almost had to run to keep up with him. His stride was no longer than ours and yet it was all we could do not to lag behind. He was never out of breath. There was such elasticity and grace, and at the same time such dignity in the way he moved!

Everything about him was remarkable: the way he held his head, his face, his gestures, and the way he looked at things; but more than anything else it was the way he walked that was striking. And as he walked he told us how to place our feet, how to breathe, how to measure each movement so as to save energy. It is important when walking to adopt a certain rhythm; in this way you gather strength as you go along, and even if you are tired when you set out, you are in fine fettle by the time you reach your destination.

The Master would draw our attention to every little detail; to him everything was important. His purpose in taking us up into the mountains was, of course, to teach us to communicate with heavenly entities through our singing, meditation and prayer, but he thought that we would learn to do so even better if we knew how to prepare our rucksack and all our equipment; how to walk and breathe; how to pause to eat and drink; how to rest... even how to wash our feet after a long climb!

Perhaps you are surprised that a Master should take the trouble to teach his disciples such trivial things. Perhaps you think that they are unworthy of his attention – especially the question of how to wash their feet! Well, you are mistaken; not only is it important to wash one's feet, it is also important to know how to do so. In the first place, it is through our feet that we are constantly in touch with the earth; it is they that pick up its currents and influences, so we must make sure that they are ready to be good receivers. Also, our feet are connected to our whole organism, particularly to the solar plexus and brain, and through them to the whole nervous system. Our head and our feet are the opposite poles of our body: through our head we are in touch with heaven, and through our feet with the earth. If we want to ensure good communications between the two poles we must work with our feet by touching them consciously and with love, talking to them and getting them to participate in our spiritual activity. As you see, every little thing is important, for every little thing can be made to contribute to our evolution.

Conditions here do not allow us to go for excursions into the mountains as we did in Bulgaria, and that is a pity. We are fortunate to be able to attend the sunrise and do our gymnastics and our breathing exercises, but these are really no substitute for a hike in the mountains. The effort spent in climbing to the top of a mountain and the relaxation that follows once the goal is reached expel all kinds of toxins from the body and leave one feeling refreshed and rejuvenated. Many people will tell you that they often go into the mountains. Yes, but they go by car. Their only effort consists in getting out of the car at a certain altitude to stretch their legs, admire the view and take a few breaths of fresh air. All the climbing is done by the car, not by them – and perhaps the car gets more benefit from it than they do!

An excursion into the mountains is truly beneficial only if you make the effort to use your own two legs. But the physical effort is not enough either. A mountain represents a rich and complex world that we still need to explore and understand, for it mirrors certain aspects of our inner life.

Mountains are links between earth and heaven. Immense wisdom went into their formation and the choice of their exact location, for this is never left to chance. Each mountain has its own particular function; this is why each one is different from all others in shape, size and height. Like antennae, their peaks point upwards, each one being specially designed to emit or receive waves of a particular frequency, thus creating conditions conducive to a particular activity. The influences exerted by the peaks of the Himalayas, Alps or Pyrenees, for instance, are not the same, and we should know which one to work with in order to obtain the desired results.

Mountains are inhabited by very luminous and powerful entities that are drawn to them by the exceptional purity that surrounds their peaks, and if we climb up to those peaks it must be in order to communicate with these entities. But this requires great knowledge, knowledge that is revealed only to those who are committed heart and soul to the path of light. Very few human beings are aware that a mountain offers extremely favourable conditions for their spiritual evolution or are capable of taking advantage of those conditions. They go to the mountains to amuse themselves, and spend their days and nights making a great deal of noise. They show no consideration or respect for the entities that dwell there. But mountains are intelligent beings, so they refuse to expose their true life to the gaze of such people. There is a danger, in fact, that the luminous entities that inhabit the mountains will eventually be so antagonized by these animals, these human beings who defile everything, that they will desert them altogether.

I was only about twenty when I had an experience which made a very deep impression on me. We were camping in the Rila mountains and I had gone with an older sister to a spot a good way above the camp. The silence up there had a sacred quality to it; it was as though no human being had ever set foot there before. We prayed and meditated and talked about the Teaching together, and then I went on a little farther to meditate alone. What happened then was quite extraordinary: the spot where I was sitting was very pretty but not more so than many other places all around, suddenly I thought I must be hallucinating, for everything around me seemed to come alive; the stones, the grass and the trees suddenly became vibrant and luminous as though by magic. The phenomenon lasted a long time, and my delight and wonder were so great I could not tear myself away from the spectacle. It was then that I realized how dreadfully ignorant we are about what nature really is. Behind her visible façade nature conceals realities such as human beings have never dreamed of; all this subtle life is hidden and unknown to them because of their stupid, noisy, unmannerly ways.

A disciple needs to go up into the mountains – not only physically but also spiritually – in order to communicate with heaven. He needs to meditate at length on what a mountain means for him, what it means in his inner life. It is a marvellous experience to climb to an altitude of three or four thousand metres, to drink the pure water of a mountain stream and bathe in a mountain lake, but it is not enough; we must extend these actions into our spiritual life.

Many expressions in our everyday lives use the imagery of mountaineering to describe something positive on the material plane. We say, for instance, that a man is at the height of his powers or has reached the peak of his profession; when someone is beginning to overcome some great difficulties we say that he is beginning to pull himself up again, and so on. And this imagery seems even more apt on the spiritual plane.

Valleys, springs, chasms, waterfalls, lakes, snow, and so on, are all rich in symbolic meaning; they all correspond to the realities of our inner life. He who meditates on a mystical or philosophical truth climbs an inner mountain, for that truth brings him closer to heaven and he is washed and vivified by the water that rises and flows within him. To strive to scale the highest peak is to cherish a high ideal, to cultivate the noblest thoughts and feelings. To fall into a chasm is to follow one's lowest, most ignoble tendencies, which end by swallowing one up. But peaks and chasms are closely related and it is worth meditating on that relationship, for the higher the peak the deeper the chasm.

The universe is represented in certain traditions as a mountain whose summit is God's inaccessible, inviolate dwelling place. The Greek gods dwelt on Mount Olympus, Moses spoke to God on Mount Sinai, and initiates have always used the symbolism of the peak or summit, even in countries where there are no real mountains.

The quest for the summit is the noblest and most significant endeavour a human being can undertake; nothing is more important. It means that he knows that he can use the powers and virtues bestowed on him by his Creator to attain heights far superior to any earthly goal. The cabbalistic symbol, the Sephirotic Tree of Life, can be seen as a mountain whose summit is the Sephirah Kether, and Kether represents omnipotence, omniscience and divine love. Great qualities are needed to reach this summit: tenacity, will-power, stability, intelligence, daring, and above all an irresistible yearning for the light and purity represented by all the Sephiroth.

A spiritual Master has to wait until a disciple has climbed to a great height before he can give him initiation and strip the blindfold from his eyes. Once he has reached a vantage point from which he is capable of understanding the architecture and overall design of the world he is ready for initiation. For this is what initiation is: the revelation that is given to one who has scaled the mountain and reached the peak.

It is very important, therefore, to understand how mountains can play a role in your evolution, and how to use them for a spiritual exercise. When you are in sight of a high mountain, even if it is very far away, stretch your hand out to it and concentrate on it mentally; speak to the entities that inhabit it, asking them for their help, and send them in return your contribution to their work. In this way you will learn to create a bond between yourself and the highest mountains and begin to draw strength and inspiration from them. Remember that mountains are condensers of energy, and that you can draw on that energy for the benefit of your family and friends and of the whole world.

You must learn to consider mountains as something sacred, for they represent the causal body of the country around them. Mont Blanc, for instance, is the causal body of France, Italy and Switzerland; Everest is the causal body of India and Tibet and the surrounding regions; Mount Musallah is the causal body of the Balkans. The physical and spiritual conditions that prevail at the tops of mountains are particularly well suited to certain kinds of psychic work; that is where you must go to formulate the desires and plans dearest to your heart. A disciple knows that by consciously scaling the heights he comes closer to his own causal body, thus making his mental work easier and more effective. I may well have known this intuitively when I was young. I first climbed Mount Musallah when I was only seventeen or eighteen, and already, in those early days, I thought of France and imagined myself taking the Master's teaching there one day. And years later what I had imagined came true; my destiny brought me to France. But it was from the peaks of Rila that I first touched your souls, long before I ever arrived here.

If you are unable to climb an actual mountain, you can at least make a practice of doing so mentally. Picture to yourself the fields and meadows you walk through; the waterfalls and rushing mountain streams you pass as you climb higher. Imagine your delight when you find edelweiss or tiny mountain roses clinging to the rocks, or when you look down on a crystal-clear lake or a dazzling expanse of snow glistening in the sun. And you must not forget when you reach the peak to speak with the utmost respect to the august entities that live there, for it is their home. Then, taking a deep breath of the pure, light air, you will find yourself soaring up into the blue sky, up into space.

Concentrate sometimes on one summit and sometimes on another; in this way you will gradually prepare yourself to make contact with the greatest spirits that have ever walked this earth, for there is a permanent relationship between the different mountain peaks and the sublime entities that visited the earth and brought light to mankind in past centuries. It is thanks to mountain peaks that we can communicate with those beings.

Then there is an exercise you can do before going to sleep at night: think of the mountains, of their forests and lakes and peaks, but also of their deep caverns and the beings who dwell in them. In this way you will always be on friendly terms with them. Mountains are more than piles of earth and rock; they are treasure houses of immense wealth in which gold, silver, crystals and precious stones are constantly being manufactured and perfected by the powerful entities entrusted with their safe-keeping. I am not saying this so that you might take it literally and go off to dig holes in the mountains in the hope of finding these treasures. I think you understand that it is the symbolic aspect of mountains that merit your attention; that it is within yourselves that you must learn to climb their heights and probe their depths.

Now, perhaps, you understand where water gets its wealth from. The highest mountains pick up waves of heavenly energy and communicate them to the earth, and the earth in turn impregnates the waters that flow within it with those energies. Water has a special fondness for mountains; it is always striving to rise to their summits, and the mountains continually send it back to the valleys. And it is because water has such an affection for mountains that we can communicate with the highest peaks by drinking water or bathing in it, for in this way we absorb some of the power that was invested in it at its source.

Chapter Eight

PHYSICAL AND SPIRITUAL WATER

Most people wash themselves, or at least their hands and face, every day. It is rightly considered to be normal behaviour for civilized people to wash. But how they wash is quite another matter. Children are told that they have to wash in order to be clean and not inconvenience others by their body odour, and that is all; it is simply a question of hygiene. But this is not enough; one can be washed and perfectly clean physically and still be as inwardly dirty as though one had never had a bath in one's life.

The physical body is not man's only body; he also has his subtle etheric, astral and mental bodies, and he has to care for them as well. He has to wash the dirt from them and cleanse them of all the impurities caused by the base sensations, desires, thoughts and feelings that he continues to harbour and nourish inwardly. Water washes us on the physical plane because it has the power to dispel and absorb impurities, and on the spiritual plane it has exactly the same power. All religions have rites of purification in which water is used – ablutions or ritual bathing, for instance – and these rites are based on an age-old lore concerning the powers of water. You will say that modern life does not lend itself particularly well to practices of this kind, but actually that is not true. From the time you get up until you go to bed you have innumerable occasions to wash, and you can make the most of these occasions when you use water to wash yourselves spiritually and psychically at the same time.

The water which we are all familiar with and with which we wash every day is a materialization of the cosmic fluid that fills the whole of space. By means of thought it is possible to be in contact with this fluid and be purified by it. The first step is to be aware, when washing, that the physical water you are touching is a spiritual element; and the first effect of that awareness will be to modify your gestures. Many people use rough, clumsy gestures when they wash, in the belief that this helps to wake them up and stimulate them and put them in a good mood. They certainly wake themselves up, but brusque, hurried gestures have a bad effect on the body, particularly on the face, for the harmony of our face comes from the extremely subtle organization of its particles along specific lines of force. Man's face is a reflection of the face of God, and those who wash their faces roughly and carelessly disturb the features of the divine image.

When you wash, therefore, try to use measured, harmonious gestures so that your thoughts may be free to do their work. Concentrate on the water, on its pure, limpid transparency, and you will soon feel that it is reaching into unknown regions within you and working its transformations. Not only will you feel lighter and purer, but your heart and mind will be nourished by new, subtler and more invigorating elements. Physical water contains all the elements and forces of spiritual water; you only have to learn to awaken them and receive them inwardly.

Initiates have various methods for exciting and enhancing the virtues of water: they mix a handful of salt in it, and light candles and burn incense while reciting certain formulas. But what is really important is to be aware that water is alive and inhabited by very pure entities. This is why, before you make contact with water, whether in your bathroom or in nature, you should greet it with great love and respect, and ask the Angel of Water to help you in your work. It is not necessary to embark on all kinds of long and complicated ceremonies in order to purify yourself. Several times a day you have the opportunity to wash in water and you should do so consciously, always remembering that the contact with physical water is simply a means of making contact with true water, that is to say, with spiritual water. To be sure, washing is something very ordinary, and we do it every day, but that is no reason to underestimate its importance. Like eating, sleeping and breathing, you should look on washing as a sacred action capable of liberating your soul. It is not enough to clean up your physical body a little and leave your subtle bodies to suffocate under thick layers of impurities. You need to open the pores of your soul and allow it to absorb all the riches contained in water.

But let us take this one step further: what are sadness, grief and discouragement? They are impurities that you have allowed to enter you and which are now attacking your psychic health, just as other toxic substances undermine your physical health. Thanks to water, however, you can overcome these things. Watch and listen to some running water – a spring, a stream or a waterfall – for running water frees the solar plexus by carrying away the elements of darkness that weigh on it. The flow of water is an image of the perpetual flow of new life; when you watch it you cannot help but be influenced by it. Of course for city-dwellers it is not easy to come across springs or waterfalls... but you can always turn on a tap! It is less poetic no doubt, but it can be just as effective; what matters is to concentrate on the water as it flows. It is also good to soak your hands in water, for all influences, both good and bad, come in and out of us through our hands; our hands, particularly the finger tips, act as antennae which pick up and transmit waves. Soak your hands in a basin of water, therefore, or hold them under a tap of running water for a few moments, with the thought that the water is flowing through you in all its freshness and purity; that it is carrying away your negative state of mind. And as it is your mental activity that is the most important element in this exercise, it is something you can always do, even when you have no water.

However difficult your circumstances in life, there is always something you can do about it. The important thing is to be active; not just to submit and do nothing. If you want to free yourself from the painful impressions that sometimes besiege you, and there is no water for you to see or touch, close your eyes and work with your imagination. In imagination you are free to take a shower or a bath, or to dive into a river, a lake or an ocean. You are free to swim or to float; to let yourself be carried away by tides or rocked by waves; to dive into the deep and lose yourself in immensity. Stay in this marvellous world of the imagination for as long as possible, and little by little a sensation of transparency and lightness will creep into you, and you will feel that you have really and truly been washed through and through by purifying, vivifying tides. Why is it that human beings, who recognize the power of water on the physical plane, seem to have not the slightest notion of its powers on the spiritual plane? You know that you can revive someone who has fainted by dashing water in his face, but it never occurs to you that spiritual water can also bring you back to life.

The exercises and methods I give you should help you to discover water inwardly. As I have often said, physical water is simply a reflection by means of which we can communicate with true water. And that true water has to be sought within us; we have to find the springs of living water that flow in the depths of our being. The work is long and difficult, I know, but one day, if you persevere, you will understand that it was this spiritual water that Jesus was referring to when he said, *'From his heart will flow rivers of living water.'*

Chapter Nine

FEEDING THE FLAME

A flame is something so fragile that the slightest breeze can extinguish it. But if you nourish a tiny flame it will become a great blaze, and the winds that once threatened its existence will fan it until it burns so fiercely that nothing can resist it. How is it that the same cause, the wind, can produce effects so diametrically opposed? The reason is simple: it is because the flame – and we – react differently to the same thing, depending on whether we are weak or strong.

A flame is a symbol of the spirit, and if you neglect it and fail to nourish it the least little difficulty will extinguish it. One meets a great many people whose spirit is dead. Oh, of course, they continue to go here and there, to amuse themselves, to tinker at their jobs and to quarrel with their neighbours, but their spirit is all but extinguished and they are so easily discouraged by the least little obstacle that they stop trying, and that is the end of them. Others, on the contrary, who have strengthened their spirit through prayer, meditation and contemplation, do not allow the obstacles they meet to impede their progress. On the contrary, they are stimulated by them; a difficulty spurs them on to further progress and they face up to the obstacles in their path with even greater ardour. In this way difficulties that defeat the weak strengthen those who are truly animated by the spirit. On the other hand, you must not simply rely on the spirit and do nothing to help yourselves on the pretext that the spirit is well armed and will always come to your rescue. No, the spirit will always be powerful and well armed only if you continue to nourish it.

Each one of you has a flame within you, and however feeble that flame may be, it is in your power to feed it until it becomes an immense blaze. But be careful how you begin; do not expose yourself to draughts that could extinguish your faith, love or hope. Do not associate with people indiscriminately; do not read anything and everything; do not indulge in any and every form of entertainment. Choose emotional, intellectual and spiritual food that will make you inwardly stronger. Once you are really strong you can stand up to anything; encounters with people or circumstances that would have destroyed you before will actually enhance your light and peace. When a fire has been fed until it is a blaze, the wind can no longer blow it out; on the contrary, it will only fan the flames to greater heights.

At this stage you will even be capable of lighting other flames and spreading the divine fire to the whole world. During the Easter celebrations in Orthodox churches, each member of the congregation lights his candle from that of the person next to him. It is as though fire were on the march, and the whole church is gradually filled with a multitude of tiny flames. In the same way, he who has succeeded in lighting his candle (his spirit) and his vigil light (his soul) at the divine flame is capable of setting the souls and spirits of those around him on fire. To be sure this can take a very long time. It may take years to achieve because he often allows too much rain and wind to enter him, but one fine day he will succeed; his candle will be alight and will begin to radiate some light around him. Seeing this, his neighbour will say, 'Ah, there is someone who can give me some light!' and will come and light his own candle. And then another and another will come, until the whole world is filled with lighted candles.

Those of you whose candle is already alight, try at least to light the candles of your children and your friends and relations. Why keep the light for yourselves alone? That is no way to bring the kingdom of God into the world. This is what you are learning here: to light and nurture the flame of your own candles so that you may also light others. And if you ever have the misfortune to extinguish the flame of your candle, you can always light it again from those that are already burning, thanks to you. One often sees this. Men and women who were deeply convinced and who had succeeded in getting others to share their convictions have sometimes been overcome by fatigue and disillusionment, but as they were caught up in a movement that they themselves had started, they could not simply abandon everything; they were carried along by others and obliged to keep going. Yes, even if the candle goes out, as long as it remains in circulation, it can be re-lit. One sometimes sees this happening with two generations of a family. The parents begin by preaching courage, self-denial and the need to stand up for a high ideal, and then they are unable to keep up their enthusiasm and begin to let things slide; but the younger generation has taken their lessons to heart, and when they are old enough to begin taking responsibility they begin to shake up their elders, carrying them along with them and rekindling their faith and their readiness to combat on the side of good.

As you see, the question has many ramifications, many far-reaching effects. This is why I tell you that you must do your best to light the candles of others with your flame and to breathe love and faith into them. In this way the fire will always burn and if one day your own flame goes out, all those whose candles you once lit will come to your rescue.

Chapter Ten

THE ESSENTIAL ROLE OF FIRE

Fire represents the boundary between the physical and the etheric planes, and this is why initiates consider it to be the most powerful means of entering into communication with the spiritual world. Before beginning an important work an initiate lights a candle, because he knows that the flame enables him to enter the subtler regions in which his voice – his thoughts – will be heard, in which he will find the conditions necessary for material realization. Every genuine magus has a very strong bond with fire. Although religion has progressively lost its understanding of these initiatic practices, the tradition of lighting candles or vigil lights in churches still exists, and this shows that, even though they may be unaware of it, human beings have preserved the ancient knowledge that fire is an earnest of realization.

It is because I know this that, when we have a ceremony of fire, I ask you to write a wish, the best possible wish, for your own evolution and the good of your friends and of the whole world; and then we give all your wishes to the Angel of Fire. Fire is the messenger of the invisible world, and when all your wishes are burned the entities of the higher world receive them and study the situation to see how to answer your requests. These entities are used to receiving so many mundane requests (some want money, others worldly success, others a husband or a wife) that they are very bored with them and also very perplexed as to how to answer them. But when they receive requests from people who ask to be perfect, to serve the Lord, to work for the kingdom of God, they pass them round in delight from one to the other and try to find ways of granting them. To be sure you must not expect your requests to be granted overnight, but if you are patient, if you persevere in your efforts and continue to work in the direction of the wish you have expressed, sooner or later it will come about, for fire always gets results.

When we are gathered round the fire like this we form a circle, of which the fire is the centre, and we must direct our thoughts and prayers towards this symbolic centre of light, warmth and life. We meet in the fire; our souls and our thoughts merge in the fire. As long as we are conscious and understand the importance of this ceremony and why we are together, everything will converge in the fire. We are gathered round this fire in order to give flesh and blood to a divine idea by enfolding it in our love and giving it the elements it needs to materialize. We must do all we can to provide our friends in the invisible world with an abundant supply of matter in which to wrap the infant, the kingdom of God, that is waiting to be born into the world.

When you know that you are going to take part in a ceremony of fire in the evening, therefore, you must try not to fritter away your energies during the day in activities that erode your magnetism. Keep your magnetism for the fire. You need all your energies in order to communicate and reach an understanding with fire. It is important for a collectivity to learn to concentrate all together on the same luminous idea, for it is then, and only then, that a ceremony of fire is potent.

The unity that reigns amongst us attracts many invisible friends. This is why, when you gather round the fire together, you must forget all your old complaints and frustrations and animosities. Try to mainfain an inner state of perfect harmony, for your state of mind is reflected by the fire; as it burns it sends back all the thoughts and feelings it has received from you. Beware of what you will receive if those thoughts and feelings were not harmonious!

Heavenly entities love harmony. You can attract them with music, songs and positive thoughts and feelings. The unity and harmony that reign amongst us when we are round the fire is such that it attracts luminous entities from every direction. For this state of harmony creates a fragrance which pervades the air; a fragrance which may not be perceived by human beings but which these luminous entities perceive at once. They say to each other, 'How different they are from other human beings who only get together to share their frustration and rage against their enemies, real or imaginary. These people are together to create unity and harmony, and to prepare the kingdom of God. Let us join them and help them.' Even the stars in the sky smile down on us and send us messages of love.

You must make friends with fire; you must contemplate it and sing for it. When you work with fire you are working for your own future. You may not see any substantial results for the moment, for spiritual work is always long and exacting, but you will be laying the groundwork and preparing the materials needed for a later materialization. In the meantime transformations will already be taking place in your consciousness; you will already sense that you have entered another dimension.

Chapter Eleven

THE CYCLE OF WATER: REINCARNATION

What is fire? Fire is water, divine water, flowing back to its source on high. Earthly water, on the other hand, does not flow back to its source; it flows down into the sea. In the long run of course, it does go back, but only when it has completed a cycle in which it is transformed and its state is changed from water to vapour. Fire, which is in the image of the spirit, does not need to go through the same transformations, because it is already pure; it returns directly to its source. The source is high up in the mountains, and water flows perpetually downwards, down towards the sea. It cannot go back to its source until it has become pure and subtle, and this is why it has to become vapour... until it is time for it to return to earth once again. And now for the interpretation of these two different journeys.

When water first gushes from a mountain spring it is pure and crystalline, but as it flows downwards it is gradually contaminated by the filth of the regions through which it passes, for all the refuse produced by men's activities eventually end up in the streams and rivers of the world. By the time it reaches the sea water is saturated with impurities. Before long, however, the sun's rays transform the sea water into vapour, and it makes its way back to the heavens until, falling back to earth in the form of rain or snow, it once again appears as springs, streams, rivers... and the cycle begins all over again.

The life cycle of water is symbolic. The destiny of human beings follows a similar cycle of countless journeys between earth and heaven. Like drops of water, human souls come down to earth and incarnate, each in a particular set of circumstances. From there each one follows its own path until, tired and worn by their labours, they return to their origins... only to come back again another day in another setting. This is what we call reincarnation.

There is a parallel, therefore, between the cycle of human reincarnation and the cycle of water; the similarities are very far-reaching. The snow that falls in the Alps or Pyrenees melts and rushes down the mountainside in torrents. As it reaches the valley it mingles with the waters of other streams and rivers and ends by flowing into the sea or the ocean. What do we know about where its journey takes it once it has been transformed into vapour? We only know that one day, depending on the winds and currents in the atmosphere, it will fall again in the form of rain, snow or hail somewhere in the world, very far perhaps from the regions it knew before. And the cycle goes on, repeating itself time after time. In the same way, when human souls reincarnate they do not find themselves in the same country or the same conditions as before.

This means that every country is like a river. The river bed is the same but the water that flows between its banks is always new; it comes from every corner of the world, and as it moves on towards the sea it is constantly followed by more new water, and so on, in a perpetual succession. Yes, a country is a river. The souls that meet and come together in it are all very different from each other, but they are there for a time in obedience to a decree of destiny. Some of them may have incarnated in that country once before, but the majority come from elsewhere.

There is an important lesson to be learned from this. When people think that their love of country entitles them to despise or even hate other countries, the poor, ignorant creatures do not realize that in a previous incarnation they were citizens of those other countries, and in those days they professed the same stupid, narrow-minded opinions about the country they defend so stoutly today. A country is our homeland only for the duration of our present incarnation. How many thousands of Frenchmen have hated Germany or England without realizing that in a previous incarnation they were English or German and hated the French! For centuries, Bulgaria, Turkey and Greece were at each other's throats; but many Greeks were reincarnations of Turks or Bulgarians, and many Bulgarians were reincarnations of Greeks or Turks. So where does that leave us? This law applies to all the countries of the world as well as to all religions. Think of how many Catholics have hated and persecuted Protestants without the slightest notion that they themselves were Protestants in a previous incarnation... and vice versa!

These considerations help us to understand that it is not the fact that we belong to a particular country or religion that matters; the soul is always on the move. You can change your country and your religion, and there will always be magnificent beings as well as criminals in both. The only thing that matters is to learn and to strive for perfection wherever you may be. And this is precisely why we keep changing countries, for in order to keep learning and growing towards perfection, human beings need to experience a variety of conditions. This is why cosmic intelligence constantly changes their circumstances. But do they understand that they have something to learn? Most human beings are loath even to hear about reincarnation. Well, that is their loss! As for you, meditate on the extraordinary lesson of the cycle of water.

Chapter Twelve

THE CYCLE OF WATER: LOVE AND WISDOM

Have you sometimes thought about the cycle that water follows in nature? It falls from the heavens and settles in the form of pure, white snow on the mountain tops, and there it stays for a while, like a sage meditating and studying in solitude and silence. It is happy to stay at this altitude, for life on the mountain tops is so vast and beautiful; there is so much room to breathe. In spite of these advantages, however, water does not stay up there for ever. Gradually, as it is warmed by the sun, it begins to flow downhill, vivifying all the creatures it meets on the way: plants, animals and human beings. Wherever it goes it works to cleanse and purify everything in its path.

But human beings are too thoughtless and ungrateful to think of thanking water for what it does for them. They use it every day in their homes and gardens, in their fields and factories; they use it to quench their thirst, cook their food, wash themselves, water their crops, and travel round the world. They also throw all their detritus into it...

but never does it occur to them to show it a little gratitude. Eventually, feeling dirty and perhaps a little sickened by such nasty, ungrateful beings, the water decides to go back to the summits, where it was once happy and free to spend all its time breathing the pure air and contemplating the splendour of the heavens. And there it stays until it feels the need to share its riches with other beings and goes down into the valleys once again.

Water has found an admirable solution to the problem of rising and descending; and you too must learn how to do this. What does this mean? It means that if you stay permanently at a high altitude, like snow on the mountain tops, you will certainly become wise and pure, but you will also be cold and proud. And you will never really be happy, for you will always be alone. From time to time you must think of going down to help others. Of course, when you go down into the valley there will be things that worry you – you will get tired and you will be spattered with impurities – but once you have done your work you will have the right to go back again to the life you love in the heights.

This is the way of a true disciple. He does not stay forever in the solitary splendour of the mountain tops, but neither does he stay too long at a time in the dust, noise and tumult of the valleys. He goes up and down; up and down. To go down is to manifest love; to go up is to seek wisdom, to study, meditate and pray. It is not good to study for too long without going down at some point to help others with one's knowledge. You must get into the habit of practising this alternation. The ascetics, hermits and recluses who fled to caves in the wilderness did not always have the best solution to this problem; but neither do those who have never scaled a mountain, that is to say, who have never felt the need of a spiritual life.

If someone goes up to the heights to study, meditate and pray and stays there too long, he will be tempted by pride, for he will feel superior to others and his heart will be hardened against them. And when this happens, who will go to visit him? A few bold mountaineers may perhaps; but after one or two attempts even they will be discouraged by his haughtiness and the cold welcome they get, and they will not go back. So he will remain alone and disenchanted, feeling that nobody understands or appreciates him. The only solution is for him to do what water does: go down into the valley.

The valleys symbolize kindness, generosity, tenderness and fertility. Trees, gardens, orchards, flowers, towns and human beings are to be found in valleys, not on the mountain tops. On mountain tops are rocks, ice and barrenness. Are you always lonely? If so, go down into the valleys where you will find abundance, where flow the rivers of love.

The learning you acquire on the mountain tops has to melt and form rivulets, streams and rivers to enrich the valleys. Your intelligence must take you up to the mountain tops, and your love must take you down into the valleys.

When you come down, of course, you will lose something and get yourself dirty. But meditate on the sacrifice of water, so innocent and transparent, which comes down to earth to take on all the impurities of human beings. You must not worry if you get a little dirty when trying to help others; you can always do as water does and blend into the ocean, for the ocean cannot be soiled. If you complain of being defiled and plundered, it is because you see yourself as a little pond... worse, as a tiny puddle of water! You must not identify with a pond; identify with the ocean, and then you will sense that you cannot be defiled by anybody or anything. And the day will come when you will be caught up by the rays of the spiritual sun, and they will take care of your purification. Rising above the earth you will leave behind all the impurities that you had absorbed along the way.

Each human being is like a drop of water, and each drop falls exactly where cosmic intelligence intended it to fall in order to accomplish its particular task. Each drop has to sacrifice itself in one way or another; some by giving drink to the thirsty; some by washing and refreshing those who are hot and dirty after the day's work; some by watering the seeds in the fields. Yes, the sacrifices required of water are numerous – we use it to make bread, cook vegetables or dissolve poisons – and it must never rebel against what is asked of it; it always has to accept. But once it has accomplished its mission it is allowed to return to the heavens and recover its transparency.

Water says, 'Do as I do. Use the twin methods of love and wisdom. Learn to go up and down, to receive and to give, and you will find fulfilment.' This is an age in which the light of the sun will shine on the snow. The snow will melt and great rivers will be formed; vegetation everywhere will be watered, and we shall see all kinds of new fruit and flowers.

Chapter Thirteen

A CANDLE FLAME

Fire symbolizes the spirit, and for this reason it has always been present in temples and churches. Sometimes it has been in the form of a great fire in an open hearth, but more often it is in the form of the little flames of candles and vigil lamps that are lit for a ceremony or left to burn as a protective presence at night. But is there still some notion of the sacredness of a flame in the minds of our contemporaries? They burn candles when the lights go out because of a power cut, or to create a festive atmosphere for a party, but they have no conception of the primeval powers they are handling and setting in motion when they light a candle.

Yes, lighting a candle is not as simple and insignificant as it seems, for in doing so you are making contact with the four elements. The candle itself, which is solid, represents earth. When you light it you have fire. Little by little the wax melts and a tiny pool of liquid forms in the hollow; and there you have water. As for air, it is always present, for it is indispensable to fire; without it the flame would die. Even if you cannot see the air, its presence is revealed by the flickering motion of the flame.

When you light a candle, therefore, try to realize that you are in the presence of the four fundamental elements of creation, and that you can work with them by linking yourself to the four great angels that govern them: the Angel of Fire, the Angel of Air, the Angel of Water and the Angel of Earth. The flame of a candle is still matter, but an extremely subtle form of matter – the subtlest that exists on the physical plane. It is animated by a force, a spirit, but it itself is matter. It is an aspect of the solar fire that illuminates, warms and vivifies us on both the physical and the spiritual planes. Obviously, on the physical plane the flame of a candle does not possess the power of solar fire, but on the spiritual plane its powers are the same. This is why it is beneficial to learn to form a bond with it.

Let me explain how you can do this. It is of course preferable to do these exercises in the evening when it is already dark. It is not much use lighting a candle in the day time, when the sun is shining. The first thing you must do before lighting your candle is to pick it up and consecrate it, saying, 'I light this candle to the glory of light, to the glory of the Angel of Fire.' You must always specify the purpose of what you are doing so that it will be properly orientated in the astral world. Everything you do with an object, all the places you take it to, leave an indelible trace on it. Even incense should be purified and consecrated to the service of God before being burned. In this way it will be reserved for the Deity; all other entities will be barred from making use of it. Through the power of the divine Word, therefore, you dedicate your candle to the glory of the Angel of Fire, then you light it and turn out all the other lights.

Gaze at the flame dancing joyfully before your eyes, so bright and lively. Admire its ardour, its movements, each shade of light and colour; the blue transparency at its base, the intensity at its heart and the brighter, clearer light at the tip. Then you can speak to the flame: 'Beloved Flame, symbol of the Holy Spirit, symbol of divine love, symbol of cosmic fire, symbol of the spiritual sun...' and ask it to penetrate deep within you, to lay a patina of fire over all your cells, so that the Holy Spirit may one day come and dwell in you. It is the fire within you that will attract the Holy Spirit. The Holy Spirit will not come into anyone who has not already done a great deal of work with the purity of fire and whose cells are not lined with light. If you want to attract the Spirit you have to become one with fire.

When fire sees that you understand the sacred nature of the flame, it will love you and help you and recognize you as a friend. It will sense that your vibrations are beginning to be in harmony with its own, and when this is the case, it no longer has the power to harm you. It is important for you to know these truths. Each major period in the history of the world is marked by the predominant influence of one of the four elements: earth, water, air or fire. Fire is going to be the predominant element in our own era; mankind will experience every form of fire. This is why we must fortify ourselves and make friends with fire, true fire, and this true fire is the sun. When we contemplate the sun and form a bond of friendship with it, the vibrations of our being gradually change until we begin to feel that we are becoming one with it. Those who love the sun and understand the place it should have in their spiritual life will be capable of withstanding the negative manifestations of fire.

Just as a single drop of water is capable of putting you in touch with the ocean, a single candle flame is capable of putting you in touch with the sun, with cosmic fire, with the Holy Spirit, whose garment is light. Gaze at the flame until you feel that you are melting into it, that you yourself are becoming flame. Love it, talk to it, make friends with it. When you are discouraged, worried or unhappy, light a candle, and by means of its flame unite yourself to all that is fire in the universe. Remind yourself that the sun is fire, that God is fire, that the Holy Spirit is fire, that everything around you is fire... this thought will restore your peace and courage. Little by little your candle will become your friend, and you will get into the habit of going to it for consolation, joy and inspiration.

In doing this you will truly feel protected, for fire is a protection. Anyone who has spent time in the desert or the bush knows that one of the most effective protections against wild animals is fire. Wild animals are terrified of fire; they sense its formidable power and know that they must keep well away. And fire plays the same role in our inner life. He who has succeeded in lighting the sacred fire within himself has the best protection against spiritual wild animals, the forces of darkness, for they sense the fire emanating from the eyes, the hands and the whole body of a genuine magus or initiate, and flee in terror.

This is what our aura is, a fire that protects us from evil spirits... on condition, of course, that it is really strong and luminous. Not all human beings have an aura capable of protecting them; they have never done anything to strengthen it, so of course it cannot prevent evil entities and pernicious influences from entering them. This is another thing you can do when you look at the flame of a candle; you can work to enhance your aura.

I know that methods like this are unfamiliar to people in the West. They may be horrified by the idea of meditating on a candle flame and of contemplating it and becoming one with it, because these activities lie beyond the realm of the intellect, and they are not used to such things. But they must realize that if they confine themselves to a western mentality, the essential reality will always elude them. They must wed East to West by learning to combine the inner and the outer reality. The spiritual life demands that we transcend the intellect, and blessed are they who manage to do this and dedicate themselves to true light. Try to open your eyes to the life you are living and compare it with the life that heaven offers you; perhaps you will decide to venture beyond what you now know.

Chapter Fourteen

HOW TO LIGHT AND TEND FIRE

What do you do when you want to light a fire in the fireplace? You begin by putting in some paper, then you lay some kindling on the paper and some bigger pieces of wood on the kindling. You strike a match and set fire to the paper; the paper communicates the fire to the kindling, and the kindling to the logs. Well, the simple fact of lighting a fire demonstrates a scientific process which also operates in our inner life. The burning match corresponds to the causal plane, the world of the spirit in which all phenomena take their origin. The match sets light to the paper (the mental plane); the paper communicates the flame to the kindling (the astral plane), which in turn sets fire to the logs (the physical plane). Everything starts in the higher spiritual world and moves down from one body to the next until it reaches the physical plane. The spark of the causal body lights the mental body; the mental body lights the astral body, and the astral body lights the physical body. It is important to understand that no true realization is possible on the physical plane unless you have started by developing the qualities of the spirit. All success in life depends on this one thing: whether or not you know how to light a fire.

First of all you receive an inspiration and this inspiration is like a spark; it is something luminous and extremely rapid, which communicates an impulse to your mental body... on condition, of course, that your mental body is capable of receiving it. On the mental level it becomes a scheme, a plan of action. Then the heart considers the plan, likes what it sees and wishes to carry it out. Finally, the will intervenes in order to set things in motion and put the plan into effect. In order to be effective and beneficial every act and every manifestation must originate in the higher divine world. It is this divine impulse that moves down to the mental plane (the realm of thought), and from there to the astral plane (the realm of feelings), clothing itself in matter that becomes gradually denser until, finally, it incarnates on the physical plane. Any course of action that is not inspired by the spirit will eventually fail, and those who embark on an activity or put their faith in their feelings, without examining the nature of the impulse that moves them, show that they do not understand how to light a fire.

Some of you may object, 'But there are all kinds of ways of lighting a fire. You do not always have to use a match.' That is true, but all the different methods hold valuable lessons for us. Think of how primitive peoples used to produce fire – and this method is still in use in some tribes even today. They rub two pieces of wood together; the friction produces heat, and when the degree of heat is sufficient a little flame appears, and behold, they have both fire and light! So, movement, heat and light. Movement is transformed into heat and heat into light.

How should we interpret this phenomenon? Well, there are certain areas of life in which human beings habitually go no further than the stage of friction, symbolically speaking. The friction produces heat, to be sure, but given the nature of that heat it never becomes light; it is more likely to become darkness. Yes, interested only in the pursuit of pleasure, most human beings look no further than the heat, that is to say, the sense of well-being they get from eating, drinking and amusing themselves. This is especially true where love and sex are concerned: all they want is the excitement and effervescence involved; they make no effort to reach some light.

You will ask, 'How can love and sexuality lead to light?' They can do so if we make the effort to master and give direction to our feelings and sensations. Sexual energy was not given to man simply for his pleasure; it is a cosmic energy, and if he learns how to work with it, it can propel him to the heights of the divine world, where the greatest secrets will be revealed to him. I have already explained this time and time again! People talk about the mystics who receive illumination... but what do you think that illumination is? It is simply the grace given to those who have succeeded in transforming the heat of their love into light.

Now, let us get back to the way we light a fire: you cannot build a fire with only one log; you have to use two or even three. Also it is no use laying them down side by side; you have to lean them together in the form of a triangle. This triangle is the symbolic representation of the three principles: heart, mind and will, or – on another plane – body, soul and spirit. For a fire to burn properly, that is to say, for life to develop harmoniously, all three are necessary.

As you see, if you meditate on how to light a fire you will find some important truths within yourselves. You will understand that if you are always frozen to the marrow it is because you have not managed to light your fire. Perhaps you could not find a match, or the wood was damp, or the paper would not burn, or you have forgotten the kindling, or you have not put your logs together correctly.

You will say, 'But why talk about fires? Our houses are heated by electricity; it is so much cleaner and easier.' That is true, of course. It is not only cleaner and easier, it is also symbolic; when you plug your heater into the electrical current you are doing symbolically exactly what an initiate does when he plugs his inner instruments directly into heavenly currents. All they have to do is press the switch and they immediately feel the life-giving warmth. Others – and that means the majority of human beings – warm themselves with wood or coal or oil, that is to say with their own feelings and emotions, and this means that they have to clean out the ashes and cinders every day and keep adding fuel to the fire. Yes, most people have to tend their fires continually, and even when they do so the results are meagre. Even when they manage to work up a great blaze by means of their unbridled passions they are still cold. And yet, from the beginning, each human being is provided with a fireplace and all the fuel he needs. It is just that most people have not got the match, the spark of the spirit, the contact with the divine world, that is needed to produce a flame.

You must sometimes have seen someone in the street who wants to smoke, and finding that he has neither matches nor a cigarette lighter, goes up to a passer-by who is smoking and asks him for a light. They put their two cigarettes end to end and the first man puffs away happily and goes on his way. And do you know why men and women feel the urge to kiss? In order to get a light from each other. Just as smokers bring their cigarettes together, a man and woman bring their lips together in order to communicate fire to each other. Sometimes the fire takes and sometimes it does not, but when it does it is sometimes so fierce that it consumes not only them and all their inner possessions, it also creates havoc all around them. To love is to give and receive fire, but it takes a great deal of knowledge to do it correctly.

Sometimes, when a fire has died down, there are still some hot coals under the ashes which can be fanned into a blaze again. Each one of you can find some hot coals hidden under the ashes and can blow on them to produce a flame within yourself, instead of trying to steal it from someone else's lips. Learn to fan your own fire so that it illuminates you and lights up the whole world. There are a great many hot embers in your souls; look for them deep down and fan them into life again, instead of always relying on a passer-by to give you a light. Meditation, prayer and breathing exercises – when they are done consciously – are all means by which you can revive your fire, and if you do this others will be able to come and light their own fires from yours.

In the temples of antiquity a sacred fire was kept burning continuously, watched over by young maidens who were known in Rome as vestal virgins. This fire symbolized the inner fire that we have constantly to feed and care for. Those who abandon themselves to their passions, who have no aspirations for what is good and true and beautiful, allow their fire to go out, and before long it can only be revived by an outside intervention. This is the state in which mankind finds itself today: it needs the initiates to intervene and rekindle its spiritual fire.

Now suppose you have stoked the fire in your fireplace to such a pitch that your room is much too hot: as it is better not to become accustomed to too much heat for fear of catching cold when you go out, you must open your windows for a moment to let in some fresh air, and also damp down your fire. How can we interpret this? It is very simple: if you have built up your inner fire too much by allowing your anger and passion to have their way, you must take steps to damp it down again, otherwise, when you go out and meet other people the contrast in temperature will be so great that your heat will be followed by a chill, which will make you ill.

To understand fire properly we also have to understand air, for they complement each other. Air brings with it an element of coolness which tempers the ardour of fire. Here again, we can find a similar phenomenon in ourselves. Man is a traveller in space; in order to fulfil his destiny, he needs both heat and cold. He carries with him his own little stove and a supply of fuel for it is cold outside and the way is long, and he needs to keep his inner fire burning. The cold that comes from outside is the air that enables him to regulate his inner temperature. Or you could say that fire is love and air is wisdom. Love is on the inside, whereas wisdom is on the outside, where it can be seen, studied and contemplated.

Many illnesses are caused by an imbalance between love and wisdom: either the inner fire is so fierce that its destructive effects are felt even on the outside, or it is so feeble that it cannot prevent the outside cold from penetrating to the inside. Think of how many people have burned up all their reserves in the few short years of their youth! They have nothing left for their years of maturity and old age. Their brains, muscles and nervous systems are no longer capable of the least little effort. All your life you have to watch over your fire and see that it is properly regulated. Observe yourselves and try to see whether you conform to the law of harmony that must reign between the inner and outer aspects.

There are people whose stoves work very well but who still feel the cold because they open their windows too often or for too long at a time; in other words, they are too cerebral. Others are ruled by their sensuality: their inner heat builds up to such a degree that the door of their stove bursts open, burning coals fall out and fire consumes everything; soon nothing is left but ashes. To fail to control the fire of your passions is the surest way of destroying all that is most precious in you. Many people seek this consuming fire, but I must warn them that they will never be able to retrieve what they lose in this way. They are like children playing with matches: they start a fire for the pleasure of watching the flames and sing for joy while everything is being reduced to ashes. Poor wretches! They do not know that this fire is always accompanied by shocks, rifts and disintegration in every part of their organism, and particularly in the brain. To be sure the effects are not immediately apparent, but something within them gradually crumbles. The trouble is, that as they are incapable of seeing how things relate to each other, they never understand that if their nervous system has become increasingly fragile, if they are thrown off balance by the least little mishap, it is because they have subjected their edifice to too many shocks.

Those who, on the contrary, avoid setting fire to things and are happier when their fire burns moderately, strengthen not only their nervous system but their whole organism. They are strong enough to face up to all the difficulties that life puts in their way. Yes, it is essential to regulate your fire; this is an absolute rule. Perhaps you are thinking, 'But it is so boring when things are not burning, when everything is quiet!' Oh, I know that you find it dull and insipid to bask in the gentle warmth of a modest fire. You think that it is only fit for cats and old people! But this simply means that you are still in the chaotic state in which the earth found itself at the beginning, when everything was still molten, still erupting and shaken by tremors. And who knows, perhaps the earth also enjoyed that state and was surprised to see how conditions gradually changed and made it possible for an organized form of life to appear.

People who are ruled by their passions are like the earth in its earliest phases of turmoil and chaos. To be sure, these inner upheavals do not prevent life from existing, but they are not conducive to the evolution of very subtle forms. A state in which a person's seething passions run riot is incompatible with the development of civilization and culture. Passionate man is a primitive world in the grip of chaos, and it is only when this world becomes calmer and more organized that plants, animals and men can begin to settle in it, and life in the truest sense of the word can exist. This is why the initiates warn us and give us advice, so that we may learn to prepare an inner world that will be fit even for angels and divinities. And when angels consent to dwell in us in the form of inspirations, intuitions and revelations, then we shall be truly happy.

If someone needs disaster or raging fires in order to feel alive it shows that he is still a primitive barbarian. Actually, you can see this throughout history: all those who put towns and villages to the torch, who burned men and women at the stake or in furnaces were barbarians. The need to burn people or things is a vestige of primitive savagery. This applies equally on the level of feelings: people who continually light the fires of passion in themselves and others are committing acts of barbarity. This behaviour is characteristic of those who have not yet learned the right way to warm themselves.

Now, if we do not want to become as cold as ice either – for this can also be a danger – we have to know how to move from the realm of the intellect to that of the heart, and reach a balance between the cold winds of wisdom and the hot winds of love. Truth is in this balance. If love is not tempered by wisdom it leads to sensuality; but wisdom without love leads to coldness, contempt and cruelty. The coldness of wisdom therefore must moderate the heat of love; and the heat of love must soften the coldness of wisdom. The temperate climate thus created is the climate most propitious to life. For a grain of wheat to develop normally it needs heat – but not too much heat – and cold – but not too much cold either. There is an ideal temperature for all the different kinds of seeds so why should there not be one for the seed that is man? Why should he be an exception?

You must take care not to let the fire get out of hand and burn up your floorboards and all your furniture, but you must not freeze by staying out in the cold of winter either. When spring comes it will bring the sunshine, and then you will not feel the need to light a fire, for it will be warm everywhere, even out of doors. When the sun shines fire senses that it is no longer needed; it has served its purpose. Speaking of Jesus, St John the Baptist said, *'He must increase but I must decrease.'* John the Baptist's role was that of a good stove! He kept souls warm during the winter that held sway before the coming of Jesus, but when Jesus came to him to be baptized John saw that the sun had risen and it was time for him to withdraw and leave Jesus to begin his mission. In the same way, in the presence of the sun of love, wisdom and truth, all the little 'stoves' of philosophers, scientists and thinkers will sense that it is time for them to withdraw. How can the mediocre have anything to say once the great sun begins to shine? Christ's true teaching is the cosmic sun. It is not yet accepted by human beings, but one day it will win all souls, and when that day comes philosophers and scientists will exclaim, 'What more can we say? The kingdom of God has arrived!' The sun will extinguish the little stoves of the proud and the fanatical. This is the sun the world needs.

In the meantime, the love that burns in many human beings is like a smoky stove which coats their inner being with soot. When this stove is kept burning and all the windows are closed the lack of air saps a person's vitality and makes him sluggish. But when the sun appears and the windows are thrown open, the fresh air comes in and he begins to revive. So stop relying so heavily on your own little stove; that is to say, on your appetites, passions, instincts and desires, for they oppose all that is most vital within you by keeping the windows of your soul closed and preventing the fresh air from entering. Never fear, you will not die of boredom if you base your life on moderation and reason! No, once the sun of wisdom and divine love begins to touch you, you will see that the gratification of your passions, which was once so important to you, has gradually come to mean nothing. Then your inner dwelling will become luminous and pure and you will know true happiness.

Chapter Fifteen

WATER, THE UNIVERSAL MEDIUM

Of the four elements, water is both the most plastic and the most absorbent. It has no form of its own; it takes the form of whatever receptacle you put it in. It has no colour of its own; it becomes red, green or yellow, depending on the terrain through which it flows. It absorbs everything therefore, the bad with the good. And since it is perpetually on the move, it carries throughout nature all the elements that it picks up on its way. This is why you have to study its itinerary and the transformations it undergoes as it passes through changing conditions.

You will perhaps say that earth too has great powers of absorption. True, but earth does not possess the fluidity and permeability of water. Air, on the other hand, cannot keep what it picks up for long; it is too mobile. Even when it is loaded with putrid, noxious fumes, it cleanses and renews itself more easily than water.

It is because of its powers of absorption and transmission that water has always had a role to play in magic rites. Many books tell of cases in which a sorcerer turned a human being into an animal – a bird or a horse for instance – after pronouncing a magic formula over a bowl of water and sprinkling the water on the victim. The *Tales of a Thousand and One Nights* include several stories of this kind. But the same properties of water can of course be used for a good purpose, as we can see from the fact that priests use water to bless the faithful. The water, which has the power to retain the currents and influences it receives, becomes the vehicle for the priest's words of blessing.

Certain traditions say that one should not leave a container of water uncovered at night, because evil entities prowl round people's houses and can leave an influence in the water, and the person who drinks it will fall ill. And one thing we know for sure, and that is that if water has been exposed to moonlight it will not have the same effect as if it had been exposed to sunlight, for the influences of sun and moon are not at all the same. Also, it is better not to drink water whose source is in the vicinity of a public wash-house, a slaughterhouse or a cemetery; and if a violent quarrel takes place anywhere near a jug of water, do not use that water to cook with, for it will have absorbed the negative vibrations created by the eruption of violence nearby. As you see then, people and circumstances can modify this universal medium, water; man can give it his physical and psychic illnesses and it will carry them away with it.

Once you understand the power of absorption of water you can use it to influence your psychic life. Think of how medicinal plants are prepared, for instance, and you will understand this phenomenon better. The properties of medicinal plants, whether healing or toxic (for there are plenty of toxic plants about, and they should be handled very carefully), need to be liberated by water. You soak or boil or steep the plants in water and then you drink the water. You do not eat the plants themselves; it is enough to drink the water in which they have soaked. This means of course that the water has absorbed all, or almost all, their healing properties. In the same way, if you are very tired you can find relief by having a bath or simply washing your hands, knowing that the water will absorb your fatigue. And if your problem is more psychic than physical, if you are worried, sad or unhappy you can apply the same remedy and the water will wash away all your cares and sorrows. On the other hand if you feel particularly happy, inspired and exalted, wait a few hours before washing even your hands. Above all, do not take a shower or a bath, for as I have said, water not only absorbs negative elements, it also absorbs positive, beneficial elements.

Water is also an excellent conductor of waves. Is there anyone amongst you who has never amused himself by throwing pebbles into water? You have all seen how concentric circles of waves spread out from the spot where your pebble fell, but how many of you have understood the phenomenon? There are other things you can do with water besides throwing pebbles, or fish-hooks or nets and catching fish, frogs... or old boots! Since it is a transmitter of waves – one of the best there is – you can use it for mental work: all you have to do is dip a finger or your whole hand into some water and concentrate on sending waves of light, love and peace out into space.

You can also infuse your drinking water with good influences. After washing your hands thoroughly, take a glass of water – preferably spring water – in your left hand and dip one or more fingers of your right hand into it while concentrating on a quality that you would like to acquire or to develop more fully. There have been many great masters of white magic who magnetized water in this way and healed the sick by giving it to them to drink. I must warn you though, that if you magnetize water in this way you must not imagine that you can use it to heal the sick. That would be very presumptuous! I only give you this method to use as an exercise. You can drink the water yourself or water your flowers with it.

Because water has such great powers of absorption and conservation it is a treasure house of innumerable secrets. The whole of the history of mankind is recorded in the rivers, lakes and oceans of the world, for everything leaves traces of its existence, and the traces of all beings, all objects and all events live on in water. It is as though water kept a negative of everything on file. The passing of a ship leaves no visible trace – the water seems to revert to exactly the same state as before – and yet the traces of that passing remain. Everything that has ever happened – naval battles, shipwrecks, and so on – is faithfully recorded exactly as it happened.

Water flows over the surface of the earth and within its depths. It flows into the sea, rises again into the atmosphere and travels through vast stretches of space. It is the supreme magic medium which permeates and impregnates the universe. If you know how to listen to a drop of water it will speak to you of the earth, the sea and the sky.

Chapter Sixteen

THE MAGIC MIRROR

Water can be compared to life itself: when it is calm, its surroundings are clearly reflected on its surface; when it is rough, the reflection is confused and unclear. But water can be much more than a smooth surface in which houses, trees or mountain peaks are reflected. In its quintessence water represents the primeval ocean that contains all creatures, *'the waters above the firmament'* of which Moses speaks in *Genesis*, when he relates how God divided the waters under the firmament from the waters above the firmament. It is the waters above the firmament that contain the archives of the universe, the cosmic library which esoteric tradition calls the Akasha Chronica. It is here that are preserved the imprints of every creature that has ever existed and of every event that has ever taken place on earth.

This is why some clairvoyants work with water; they look into a bowl of water in order to 'see'. It is not that they actually see something in the water, but through it they are in touch with the waters above and with the images floating in those waters. In this way their spirit finds what they are looking for. Others prepare a magic mirror by filling a glass sphere with water that has been carefully prepared in advance for the purpose. Actually, the crystal ball that many mediums use is simply another form of water. It is true that some clairvoyants can see images in fire, but that is more rare; clairvoyance is more often associated with water. In fact those who live close to water, by the seashore or near a river or lake, often end by developing a form of clairvoyance.

Esoteric literature has many tales to tell of strange experiments. One of these concerns the preparation of a liquor known as *'spiritus universalis'*, which is a mixture of rain-water, dew and melted snow. He who possesses this liquor can determine from afar another person's state of health as well as many other details about him. He can also sprinkle the ashes of a plant with it and it will appear again on the etheric plane. Even if the plant has been dead for thousands of years, he will see it as it once was. The *spiritus universalis* enables one to take a remnant of anything at all, and see it as it originally appeared. The apparition does not last long, but one can renew it as often as one likes.

I mention these things only to give you some idea of what is possible, not in order to encourage you to do similar experiments of your own, for they are of no real use for the spiritual life. When I talk to you about magic mirrors and clairvoyance, my principal concern is the inner work you can do with water in order to purify yourselves and enhance your sensitivity in relation to the divine world.

Many years ago I invited you into my garden at the Bonfin, and gave each one of you some water that I had prepared especially for you by consecrating it to the Angel of Water. The Angel of Water was there with us, accompanied by his attendants, a multitude of magnificent spirits; and when you drank the water, these beings entered into you. Today that water is still working within you, working to cleanse your etheric and astral bodies of impure elements which obstruct the passage of celestial currents. It is like a baptism: you have been consecrated and marked with the seal of the Angel of Water. My hope is that you will show yourselves to be worthy of it by preserving and consciously amplifying what you received with that water.

Little by little you will get to know other friends in the higher world. In the rites of initiation in olden times, the hierophants presented their disciples to the luminous entities of the invisible world, asking them to take charge of them and work on them. And you too have been presented to some very powerful entities: not only to the Angel of Water, but also to the Angel of Fire, and the Archangel of the Sun. Henceforth you are under their protection.

Meditate on water. When you pour yourself a glass of water get into the habit of holding the glass in your hand for a few seconds before drinking, and say, 'I greet you, good, pure, living water, faithful servant of God; I ask you to instil purity into me.' When you do this you will feel a subtle fluid impregnating your whole being. Look at the water and identify with it. Imagine that you have the same transparency, the same crystalline translucence. Little by little, water will no longer be simply the colourless, insignificant liquid you cook and wash with; you will feel the source of all wonders opening within you. People and things will reveal themselves to you as they are in reality, behind the veil of their outward appearance.

Water is a reflection of the universal soul, that etheric substance in which all creatures are immersed and in which everything is recorded. And our own soul is a particle of the universal soul, but we rarely receive the messages the universal soul sends us because our psychic channels of communication are blocked up. But someone who has worked long and perseveringly to purify himself can rise to the level of this heavenly water and receive marvellous images in his soul.

Learn to love water. Fill a bowl with pure water and gaze at it while conjuring up in your mind the most poetic and luminous images of nature. It is possible that you will actually see these images in the water, this true magic mirror, but the important thing is to feel their living presence in your own being, for that presence is a nourishment for your soul.

Chapter Seventeen

TREES OF LIGHT

There are several different kinds of fuel we can use in our fires. For a very long time wood was the only fuel men knew, until coal was discovered. Coal produces greater heat than wood, but it also produces more dust and cinders, and its emanations, the influences it gives off, are less subtle than those of wood and do not have the same pleasant fragrance. The emanations of a wood fire are better for your health and its flames induce a better frame of mind. As for the various heating appliances in use today, they are certainly very useful and very efficient, but the heat they produce does not possess the virtues of the living heat from a wood fire.

From my earliest years I have always loved fire; I felt instinctively that its effects were beneficial. When I had a bad cold or a fever I would light a fire in the wood stove, and settling down beside it, I would gaze into it with a feeling of love and gratitude for its warmth until I fell asleep; and when I woke up I was cured. This was how I learned that a wood fire had healing properties; that the living energy of trees can be transformed into health and vigour. It is not only the heat; there are other elements in a wood fire that give it its power to heal. To be sure fire cannot cure all illnesses, but it can give us, as it were, a transfusion of energy.

Why do people who approach a fire instinctively hold out their hands to it? There is a reason for this: the ends of our fingers are equipped with many very sensitive cells, and when we hold our hands out to a fire, the sensitive centres in the tips of our fingers and the palms of our hands are stimulated and begin to function. They receive the light and heat and other subtle elements emanating from the fire and communicate them to the whole body. Old people are particularly fond of a fire, for their own warmth is gradually deserting them. They will happily sit by a fire all day long, feeding the flames and keeping it alive, gazing into it and dozing off from time to time, and holding out their hands to its heat. They sense that the fire gives them something of its own life. Yes, and the reason why the life contained in a wood fire is so precious is that it comes from the sun.

A tree is a living creature which knows not only how to absorb and store up solar energy, but also how to fix the molecules of air, water and earth that contribute to the formation of its roots, trunk and branches. It is also capable of giving these elements an appearance of solidity, strength, height and breadth, which seems to have no relation to the light, air, water and earth from which they came. But if you burn a tree you will see these great trunks and branches disintegrating before your eyes, and once the flames have died down and the gasses and water vapour have disappeared into the atmosphere, all that is left on the ground are a few handfuls of ash that weigh almost nothing.

What does this ash consist of ? It is all that is left of the element earth, thanks to which the particles of water, air and light welded themselves together to form a tree. Subtle energies cannot be fixed without the help of a material support. A tree is capable of storing up all those rays of sunlight, all those subtle elements it receives day after day, only because it possesses the matter which serves to fix them, and that matter is what we call earth. A tree, therefore, is a being that is more spiritual than material. It consists of a small proportion of earth, a larger proportion of water, and an even larger proportion of air; but it is fire, light, that constitutes the major part of a tree.

Man is built on the same principle as a tree: if his body is burned after death, as is the custom in many countries, his ashes can all be put in one little urn. Those ashes are all that is left of the matter that served to fix the fire, the sun's rays. Man then is made of fire, of light; he possesses the same quintessence as the sun. Why do people have to be misled by being taught that they are earth, that the only nourishment they need is material, and that they will return to earth? Initiates tell us, on the contrary, that we are light, that we can be nourished by light, and that we shall return to light. Yes, man is exactly like a tree, and if he understood the laws of nature, he too could fix and store up these cosmic forces, this celestial energy... that is to say, all the forms of the spirit which we call intelligence, light and love.

Watch a fire as it burns. Fire teaches us to detach ourselves from all that is material and coarse, from our own outer envelopes and husks. All that accumulation of solar energy, which is the soul of the tree, resumes its original form as it frees itself and returns to the heavenly regions. The soul of the tree is going home, and it is fire that helps it to break out of its prison by unlocking the myriad openings through which it will escape. The crackling and sputtering we hear is the language of liberation. When the opening is too narrow, the soul has to pound on the prison walls and force its way through and the explosions we hear are the soul's song of victory as it frees itself.

Look at those threads of light darting up from the fire; for only a few seconds they flash through the night before being extinguished. One has the impression that they are weaving something, as though all your prayers to the Angel of Fire were weaving a garment of light. And those plumes and bouquets of sparks... just look at them. They are an image of the millions of seeds a man releases into the depths of a woman to fertilize her. All those sparks flying out into space are going to fertilize a multitude of beings and give to some spirits the means to incarnate. For fire is a tree which produces an abundance of seeds, and those seeds in turn produce other trees. Every now and then the flames seem to take on the forms and movements of leaves and branches, it is as though, to the end, the tree were trying to preserve some element of what it once was. Before disappearing completely it reveals all the beauty of its sacrifice in this foliage of light.

Fire devours the tree and transforms it into itself. The tree becomes fire, because fire consumes it. This is a law: everything, every living being becomes identical to the one who consumes it. And this is true for us too: if we give our whole being to the fire of divine love and beg it to take us and devour us, it will transform us into itself. We all have enough material in us to feed the flames of divine love for all eternity. This is why we should meditate on fire and try to understand how it works on a tree and transforms it into light and heat, so that we too may become trees of light.

There are people who are capable of walking and dancing on hot coals. Fire does not hurt them because it recognizes them as its friends. They recite special prayers and magic formulas while making certain gestures, and then they sing as they dance on the coals, and the fire leaves them unharmed. Of course I do not advise you to try this! Be content with the exercises I have given you; they are absolutely safe. They will not make you capable of pitting yourself against fire, but they will help you to feel stronger, more alive, and more lucid and serene.

Chapter Eighteen

THE COMING OF THE HOLY SPIRIT

Initiation is the inner path that a human being has to follow to reach the goal of fire. But what is this fire? It is of course a psychic, spiritual phenomenon. Actually you could say that there are two kinds of fire: the astral fire of man's lower appetites which leads to great suffering and ends by consuming his whole being; and the spiritual fire which frees man from his imperfections and weaknesses and brings out in him all that is pure and noble. All human beings are familiar with astral fire, the fire of passion and cupidity, and especially the fire of that avid, selfish sexual love which can plunge men and women into the torments of hell. With cries of joy, astral fire pounces on them and devours them, for it sees that they are ripe and ready to be eaten; and of course they suffer and cry out in agony before being very quickly reduced to smoke and ashes.

Celestial fire, on the other hand, seeks out those who tread the path of purity, selflessness and sacrifice, and it too pounces on them and embraces them, but it does so in order to transform them into beings of light. For – and it is important to know this – divine fire never destroys something that is of the same nature as itself. When it enters man the only thing it burns are his impurities; that which is pure is not destroyed by this fire; on the contrary, it becomes luminous because it vibrates in unison with it.

This then is the task of a disciple: to attract celestial fire into himself. But he knows that this fire will come only when a place has been prepared for it, so he works tirelessly to purify and sanctify this place within himself. By means of meditation, prayer, and the daily practice of the virtues, he builds a dwelling of pure, luminous matter to which celestial fire is drawn because it recognizes in it its own quintessence. In the Christian tradition this heavenly fire is called the Holy Spirit, and the feast of Pentecost celebrates the coming of the Holy Spirit on Jesus' disciples in the form of flames or tongues of fire. On that day they received the gifts of healing, prophecy and tongues, for the Holy Spirit never comes alone; he is always accompanied by angels and archangels, by a whole heavenly hierarchy, and by a host of servants of nature who make their dwelling in man in the form of gifts, talents and virtues.

Visible fire is a material reflection of the invisible fire. This is why, every time we light a visible fire, we should remember to unite our souls and spirits to the celestial fire which is love, intelligence and power, which is in other words the Holy Spirit. What is the use of lighting a candle if you do not do this? And when celestial fire sees someone who is drawn to it, who loves and understands it, it too feels drawn to that person. This is why celestial fire has been compared to a lover, a bridegroom who embraces his beloved.

This same image is found in the Gospel parable of the wise and foolish virgins. *'Then the kingdom of Heaven shall be likened to ten virgins who took their lamps and went out to meet the bridegroom. Five of them were wise and five were foolish. Those who were foolish took their lamps and took no oil with them, but the wise took oil in their vessels with their lamps. But while the bridegroom was delayed, they all slumbered and slept. And at midnight a cry was heard, Behold, the bridegroom is coming; go out to meet him! Then all those virgins arose and trimmed their lamps. And the foolish said to the wise, Give us some of your oil, for our lamps are going out. But the wise answered, saying, No, lest there should not be enough for us and you; but go rather to those who sell, and buy for yourselves. And while they went to buy, the bridegroom came, and those who were ready went in with him to the wedding; and the door was shut.'*

This parable has meaning only if you see that the bridegroom for whom the virgins were waiting symbolizes the Holy Spirit, and the wise and foolish virgins represent the souls of human beings, both men and women. Jesus used the term 'virgin' because the soul is a feminine principle which, like a virgin, must make itself ready for the coming of the bridegroom, the Spirit. And since the Holy Spirit is a fire, how can the soul attract it if it has no oil with which to feed its flame? The Holy Spirit is a cosmic principle, to be sure, but even the Holy Spirit eats and if you try to starve it, it will simply not come to you. It is up to the soul, therefore, to prepare the oil with which to feed the flame of the Spirit. How? By cultivating purity, love, kindness, justice and wisdom, for it is these virtues that nourish the bridegroom. As long as the soul has this oil, it will be able to attract and hold the affections of the Holy Spirit.

To my mind nothing is more precious or more rare; no grace can be compared to the coming of the Holy Spirit. It is like a bolt of heavenly lightning; there is nothing more sublime. But when someone has been struck by this celestial lightning, that does not immediately make him omniscient, omnipotent and perfect. Not at all. It simply gives him the possibility to become perfect; it is up to him to work with the fire he has received. Unfortunately he can also lose this grace, lose the Holy Spirit, and this is the most terrible loss any human being can suffer. Many spiritualists, mystics and initiates, who once possessed this fire, have lost it in one way or another. Some of them managed to recover it, but at the price of what suffering, labours and tears of repentance! They had to plead with the utmost humility for a long time before the fire agreed to return to them. But once the heavenly fire returns to someone, it clings to them so stubbornly and thrusts its roots so deeply into their being that it can no longer leave them. From that moment it guides, controls and orientates the person's life and he becomes a tabernacle of the Most High; as the years go by he manifests himself more and more divinely.

I have always had a special affection for fire and have had innumerable experiences with it. Every day I am constantly engaged in conversation with fire. Both inwardly and outwardly, fire is the only thing that truly interests me; divine fire and the sun, which is its most faithful expression for us here on earth. This is why it is so important to contemplate the sun as it rises every morning, so as to renew the contact with heavenly fire. It is the sun that reveals to us the mystery of fire, the mystery of the Holy Spirit. Bind yourself to the sun with the bonds of love and intelligence and keep advancing tirelessly towards it. For initiation is the path that a human being has to follow to reach this fire.

Chapter Nineteen

A TREASURY OF PICTURES

Get into the habit of watching and listening to the life of nature, to the life of stones, plants and animals, and above all to the four elements in whatever form they may appear: rocks, sand, rain, snow, wind, sun, stars, and so on. There are so many things all around for you to observe and interpret, but you never pay any attention to them and the result is that you are living in a world whose reality is completely unknown to you. You are immersed in it every day of your life, but it is still foreign to you; you do not understand the language it speaks.

Look at all the different forms and colours of clouds, for instance. All the cavalcades, battles and fiestas we see in the clouds are the spirits of the air at work. The skies are teeming with life, and this life expresses itself in a multitude of forms: faces, birds, flocks of sheep and landscapes. There is even a form of writing, and it does not matter if we are incapable of deciphering it; the only thing that matters is consciously to allow ourselves to be impregnated by all these images.

This was how wise men of old learned the secrets of nature: they would pause by a spring, for example, and stay for a long time, watching it and listening to the murmur of the flowing water, so fresh, so crystal-clear, so alive! In this way they were gradually in communion with the soul of water, the soul of the spring. And you can do the same with fire: learn how to look at it. Even if you have the impression that you understand nothing, it does not matter. What matters is to be open to its voice, for it is in this way that you prepare your subtle centres that will, one day, be your means of contact with the life of nature.

All the ideas, impressions, sensations and mental images that occur to us leave a trace, a permanent imprint in our being. Our psychic life is shaped and moulded every day by the forces and influences we allow to enter and impregnate us. This is why it is essential to have a store of lovely pictures that we can conjure up in our minds often; pictures that are with us day and night, so that our thoughts may be constantly in touch with all that is most elevated, pure and sacred. And what is more beautiful, more poetic or more full of meaning than water and fire and the different forms in which they appear to us?

You can fill your whole life with these pictures and absorb them until they impregnate every cell of your body. If you had nothing but the presence of fire and water with which to nourish your spiritual life, it would still be enough. If you concentrate every day on these mental pictures, they will vivify, purify and illuminate you.

By the same author:

Izvor Collection

201 - Toward a Solar Civilization

It is not enough to be familiar with the astronomical theory of heliocentricity. Since the sun is the centre of our universe, we must learn to put it at the centre of all our preoccupations and activities.

202 - Man, Master of His Destiny

If human beings are to be masters of their own destiny, they must understand that the laws which govern their physical, psychic and spiritual life are akin to those which govern the universe.

203 - Education Begins Before Birth

Humanity will improve and be transformed only when people realize the true import of the act of conception. In this respect, men and women have a tremendous responsibility for which they need years of preparation.

204 - The Yoga of Nutrition

The way we eat is as important as what we eat. Through our thoughts and feelings, it is possible to extract from our food spiritual elements which can contribute to the full flowering of our being.

205 - Sexual Force or the Winged Dragon

How to master, domesticate and give direction to our sexual energy so as to soar to the highest spheres of the spirit.

206 - A Philosophy of Universality

We must learn to replace our restricted, self-centred point of view with one that is immensely broad and universal. If we do this we shall all benefit; not only materially but particularly on the level of consciousness.

207 - What is a Spiritual Master

A true spiritual Master is, first, one who is conscious of the essential truths written by cosmic intelligence into the great book of Nature. Secondly, he must have achieved complete mastery of the elements of his own being. Finally, all the knowledge and authority he has acquired must serve only to manifest the qualities and virtues of selfless love.

208 - The Egregor of the Dove or the Reign of Peace

Peace will finally reign in the world only when human beings work to establish peace within themselves, in their every thought, feeling and action.

209 - Christmas and Easter in the Initiatic Tradition

Human beings are an integral part of the cosmos and intimately concerned by the process of gestation and birth going on in nature. Christmas and Easter – rebirth and resurrection – are simply two ways of envisaging humanity's regeneration and entry into the spiritual life.

210 - The Tree of the Knowledge of Good and Evil

Methods, not explanations, are the only valid answers to the problem of evil. Evil is an inner and outer reality which confronts us every day, and we must learn to deal with it.

211 - Freedom, the Spirit Triumphant

A human being is a spirit, a spark sprung from within the Almighty. Once a person understands, sees and feels this truth, he will be free.

212 - Light is a Living Spirit

Light, the living matter of the universe, is protection, nourishment and an agency for knowledge for human beings. Above all, it is the only truly effective means of self-transformation.

213 - Man's Two Natures, Human and Divine

Man is that ambiguous creature that evolution has placed on the borderline between the animal world and the divine world. His nature is ambivalent, and it is this ambivalence that he must understand and overcome.

214 - Hope for the World: Spiritual Galvanoplasty

On every level of the universe, the masculine and feminine principles reproduce the activity of those two great cosmic principles known as the Heavenly Father and the Divine Mother of which every manifestation of nature and life are a reflection. Spiritual galvanoplasty is a way of applying the science of these two fundamental principles to one's inner life.

215 - The True Meaning of Christ's Teaching

Jesus incorporated into the Our Father - or Lord's Prayer - an ancient body of knowledge handed down by Tradition and which had existed long before his time. A vast universe is revealed to one who knows how to interpret each of the requests formulated in this prayer.

216 - The Living Book of Nature

Everything in nature is alive and it is up to us to learn how to establish a conscious relationship with creation so as to receive that life within ourselves.

217 - New Light on the Gospels

The Parables and other tales from the Gospels are here interpreted as situations and events applicable to our own inner life.

218 - The Symbolic Language of Geometrical Figures

Each geometrical figure – circle, triangle, pentagram, pyramid or cross – is seen as a structure fundamental to the organization of the macrocosm (the universe) and the microcosm (human beings).

219 - Man's Subtle Bodies and Centres

However highly developed our sense organs, their scope will never reach beyond the physical plane. To experience richer and subtler sensations, human beings must exercise the subtler organs and spiritual centres that they also possess: the aura, the solar plexus, the Hara centre, the Chakras, and so on.

220 - The Zodiac, Key to Man and to the Universe

Those who are conscious of being part of the universe feel the need to work inwardly in order to find within themselves the fullness of the cosmic order so perfectly symbolized by the Zodiac.

221 - True Alchemy or The Quest for Perfection

Instead of fighting our weaknesses and vices – we would inevitably be defeated – we must learn to make them work for us. We think it normal to harness the untamed forces of nature, so why be surprised when a Master, an initiate, speaks of harnessing the primitive forces within us? This is true spiritual alchemy.

222 - Man's Psychic Life: Elements and Structures

"Know thyself." How to interpret this precept carved over the entrance to the temple at Delphi? To know oneself is to be conscious of one's different bodies, from the denser to the most subtle, of the principles which animate these bodies, of the needs they induce in one, and of the state of consciousness which corresponds to each.

223 - Creation: Artistic and Spiritual

Everyone needs to create but true creation involves spiritual elements. Artists, like those who seek the spirit, have to reach beyond themselves in order to receive elements from the higher planes.

224 - The Powers of Thought

Thought is a power, an instrument given to us by God so that we may become creators like himself – creators in beauty and perfection. This means that we must be extremely watchful, constantly verifying that what we do with our thoughts is truly for our own good and that of the whole world. This is the one thing that matters.

225 - Harmony and Health

Illness is a result of some physical or psychic disorder. The best defence against illness, therefore, is harmony. Day and night we must take care to be attuned and in harmony with life as a whole, with the boundless life of the cosmos.

226 - The Book of Divine Magic

True, divine magic, consists in never using the faculties, knowledge, or powers one has acquired for one's own self-interest, but always and only for the establishment of God's kingdom on earth.

227 - Golden Rules for Everyday Life

Why spoil one's life by chasing after things that matter less than life itself? Those who learn to give priority to life, who protect and preserve it in all integrity, will find more and more that they obtain their desires. For it is this, an enlightened, luminous life that can give them everything.

228 - Looking into the Invisible

Meditation, dreams, visions, astral projection all give us access to the invisible world, but the quality of the revelations received depends on our efforts to elevate and refine our perceptions.

229 - The Path of Silence

In every spiritual teaching, practices such as meditation and prayer have only one purpose: to lessen the importance attributed to one's lower nature and give one's divine nature more and more scope for expression. Only in this way can a human being experience true silence.

230 - The Book of Revelations: A Commentary

If *Revelations* is a difficult book to interpret it is because we try to identify the people, places and events it describes instead of concentrating on the essence of its message: a description of the elements and processes of our spiritual life in relation to the life of the cosmos.

231 - The Seeds of Happiness

Happiness is like a talent which has to be cultivated. Those who want to possess happiness must go in search of the elements which will enable them to nourish it inwardly; elements which belong to the divine world.

232 - The Mysteries of Fire and Water

Our psychic life is fashioned every day by the forces we allow to enter us, the influences that impregnate us. What could be more poetic, more meaningful than water and fire and the different forms under which they appear?

233 - Youth: Creators of the Future

Youth is full of life, enthusiasms and aspirations of every kind. The great question is how to channel its extraordinary, overflowing effervescence of energies.

234 - Truth, Fruit of Wisdom and Love –

We all abide by our own "truth", and it is in the name of their personal "truth" that human beings are continually in conflict. Only those who possess true love and true wisdom discover the same truth and speak the same language.

235 - In Spirit and in Truth

Since we live on earth we are obliged to give material form to our religious beliefs. Sacred places and objects, rites, prayers and ceremonies are expressions of those beliefs. It is important to understand that they are no more than expressions – expressions which are always more or less inadequate. They are not themselves the religion, for religion exists in spirit and in truth.

236 - Angels and Other Mysteries of the Tree of Life

God is like a pure current of electricity which can reach us only through a series of transformers. These transformers are the countless luminous beings which inhabit the heavens and which tradition calls the Angelic Hierarchies. It is through them that we receive divine life; through them that we are in contact with God.

237 - Cosmic Balance, the Secret of Polarity

Libra - the Scales - symbolizes cosmic balance, the equilibrium of the two opposite and complementary forces, the masculine and feminine principles, by means of which the universe came into being and continues to exist. The symbolism of Libra, expression of this twofold polarity, dominates the whole of creation.

238 - The Faith That Moves Mountains

Faith is the result of an age-old knowledge buried deep within our subconscious. It is founded on an experience of the divine world, an experience which has left indelible traces on each one of us and which we must reanimate.

239 - Love Greater Than Faith

As long as we have not understood what true faith is, there can be no love; and conversely, as long as we do not know how to manifest love, we cannot claim that we have faith.

Books by Omraam Mikhaël Aïvanhov

(translated from the French)

Complete Works

Volume 1 – The Second Birth
Volume 2 – Spiritual Alchemy
Volume 5 – Life Force
Volume 6 – Harmony
Volume 7 – The Mysteries of Yesod
Volume 10 – The Splendour of Tiphareth
The Yoga of the Sun
Volume 11 – The Key to the Problems of Existence
Volume 12 – Cosmic Moral Laws
Volume 13 – A New Earth
Methods, Exercises, Formulas, Prayers
Volume 14 – Love and Sexuality (Part I)
Volume 15 – Love and Sexuality (Part II)
Volume 17 – 'Know Thyself' Jnana Yoga (Part I)
Volume 18 – 'Know Thyself' Jnana Yoga (Part II)
Volume 25 – A New Dawn:
Society and Politics in the Light of Initiatic Science (Part I)
Volume 26 – A New Dawn:
Society and Politics in the Light of Initiatic Science (Part II)
Volume 29 – On the Art of Teaching (Part III)
Volume 30 – Life and Work in an Initiatic School
Training for the Divine
Volume 32 – The Fruits of the Tree of Life
The Cabbalistic Tradition

Brochures

301 – The New Year
302 – Meditation
303 – Respiration
304 – Death and the Life Beyond

World Wide - Editor-Distributor

Editions PROSVETA S.A. - B.P. 12 - F- 83601 Fréjus Cedex (France)

Tel. (00 33) 04 94 19 33 33 - Fax (00 33) 04 94 19 33 34

Web: **www.prosveta.com**

e-mail: **international@prosveta.com**

Distributors

AUSTRALASIA

SURYOMA LTD - P.O. Box 2218 – Bowral – N.S.W. 2576 Australia
e-mail: info@suryoma.com – Tel. (61) 2 4872 3999 – fax (61) 2 4872 4022

AUSTRIA

HARMONIEQUELL VERSAND – A- 5302 Henndorf am Wallersee, Hof 37
Tel. / fax (43) 6214 7413 – e-mail: info@prosveta.at

BELGIUM & LUXEMBOURG

PROSVETA BENELUX – Liersesteenweg 154 B-2547 Lint
Tel (32) 3/455 41 75 – Fax (32) 3/454 24 25 – e-mail: prosveta@skynet.be
N.V. MAKLU Somersstraat 13-15 – B-2000 Antwerpen
Tel. (32) 3/231 29 00 – Fax (32) 3/233 26 59
VANDER S.A. – Av. des Volontaires 321 – B-1150 Bruxelles
Tél. (32)(0)2 732 35 32 – Fax. (32) (0)2 732 42 74 – e-mail: g.i.a@wol.be

BULGARIA

SVETOGLED – Bd Saborny 16 A, appt 11 – 9000 Varna
e-mail: svetgled@revolta.com – Tel/Fax: (359) 52 23 98 02

CANADA

PROSVETA Inc. – 3950, Albert Mines – Canton-de-Hatley (Qc), J0B 2C0
Tel. (819) 564-8212 – Fax. (819) 564-1823
in Canada, call toll free: 1-800-854-8212
e-mail: prosveta@prosveta-canada.com / www.prosveta-canada.com

COLUMBIA

PROSVETA – Calle 149 N° 24 B - 20 – Bogotá
Tel. (57) 1 614 88 28 – Fax (57) 1 633 58 03 – Mobile (57) 310 2 35 74 55
e-mail: kalagiya@tutopia.com

CYPRUS

THE SOLAR CIVILISATION BOOKSHOP – BOOKBINDING
73 D Kallipoleos Avenue - Lycavitos – P. O. Box 24947, 1355 – Nicosia
e-mail: cypapach@cytanet.com.cy – Tel / Fax 00357-22-377503

CZECH REPUBLIC

PROSVETA – Ant. Sovy 18, – České Budejovice 370 05
Tel / Fax: (420) 38-53 10 227 – e-mail: prosveta@iol.cz

GERMANY

PROSVETA Deutschland – Heerstrasse 55 – 78628 Rottweil
Tel. (49) 741-46551 – Fax. (49) 741-46552 – e-mail: prosveta.de@t-online.de

GREAT BRITAIN – IRELAND

PROSVETA – The Doves Nest, Duddleswell Uckfield, – East Sussex TN 22 3JJ
Tel. (44) (01825) 712988 - Fax (44) (01825) 713386
e-mail: prosveta@pavilion.co.uk

GREECE

RAOMRON – D. RAGOUSSIS
3, rue A. Papamdreou – C.P. 16675 – Glifada - Athenes
Tel / Fax: (010) 9681127 – e-mail: raomron@hol.gr

HAITI

PROSVETA – DÉPÔT – B.P. 115, Jacmel, Haiti (W.I.)
Tel./ Fax (509) 288-3319
e-mail: haiti@prosveta.com

HOLLAND

STICHTING PROSVETA NEDERLAND
Zeestraat 50 – 2042 LC Zandvoort
Tel. (31) 33 25 345 75 – Fax. (31) 33 25 803 20
e-mail: prosveta@worldonline.nl

ISRAEL

Zohar, P. B. 1046, Netanya 42110
e-mail: zohar7@012.net.il

ITALY

PROSVETA Coop. a r.l. – Casella Postale 55 – 06068 Tavernelle (PG)
Tel. (39) 075-835 84 98 – Fax (39) 075-835 97 12
e-mail: prosveta@tin.it

LIBAN

PROSVETA LIBAN – P.O. Box 90-995
Jdeidet-el-Metn, Beirut – Tel. (03) 448560
e-mail: prosveta_lb@terra.net.lb

NORWAY

PROSVETA NORDEN – Postboks 318, N-1502 Moss
Tel. (47) 69 26 51 40 – Fax (47) 69 25 06 76
e-mail: prosnor@online.no

PORTUGAL & BRAZIL

EDIÇÕES PROSVETA
Rua Passos Manuel, n° 20 – 3e E, P 1150 – 260 Lisboa
Tel. (351) (21) 354 07 64 – Fax (351) (21) 798 60 31
e-mail : prosvetapt@hotmail.com
PUBLICAÇÕES EUROPA-AMERICA Ltd
Est Lisboa-Sintra KM 14 – 2726 Mem Martins Codex

ROMANIA

ANTAR – Str. N. Constantinescu 10 - Bloc 16A - sc A - Apt. 9,
Sector 1 – 71253 Bucarest
Tel. 004021-231 28 78 - Tel./ Fax 004021-231 37 19
e-mail : antared@pcnet.ro

RUSSIA

EDITIONS PROSVETA
143 964 Moskovskaya oblast, g. Reutov – 4, post/box 4
Tel./ Fax. (095) 525 18 17 – Tél. (095) 795 70 74
e-mail: prosveta@online.ru

SPAIN

ASOCIACIÓN PROSVETA ESPAÑOLA – C/ Ausias March n° 23 Ático
SP-08010 Barcelona – Tel (34) (93) 412 31 85 - Fax (34) (93) 318 89 01
aprosveta@prosveta.es

UNITED STATES

PROSVETA US Dist.
PO Box 2125 – Canyon Country CA 91386
Tél. (661)252-1751 – Fax. (661) 252-9090
e-mail: prosveta_usa@earthlink.net / www.prosveta-usa.com

SWITZERLAND

PROSVETA Société Coopérative
Ch. de la Céramone 3A – CH - 1808 Les Monts-de-Corsier
Tél. (41) 21 921 92 18 – Fax. (41) 21 922 92 04
e-mail: prosveta@swissonline.ch

VENEZUELA

PROSVETA VENEZUELA C. A. – Calle Madrid
Edificio La Trinidad – Las Mercedes – Caracas D.F.
Tel. (58) 414 22 36 748 – e-mail : betty_mramirez@hotmail.com

The aim of the Universal White Brotherhood association
is the study and practice of the Teaching
of Master Omraam Mikhaël Aïvanhov,
published and distributed
by Prosveta.

All enquiries about the association should be addressed to:
Universal White Brotherhood
The Doves Nest, Duddleswell, Uckfield
East Sussex TN22 3JJ, GREAT BRITAIN
Tel: (44) (0)1825 712150 – Fax: (44) (0)1825 713386
E-mail: uwb@pavilion.co.uk

Printed in September 2004
by DUMAS-TITOULET Imprimeurs
42004 Saint-Etienne – France

Dépôt légal : Septembre 2004
Imprimeur : 41048C
1er dépôt légal dans la même collection: 1993